Shadows of the Crimson Sun

One Man's Life in Manchuria, Taiwan, and North America

Julia Lin

MAWEN**Z**I
HOUSE

We acknowledge the support of the Canada Council for the Arts for our publishing program. We also acknowledge support from the Government of Ontario through the Ontario Arts Council.

Cover design by Sabrina Pignataro
Cover photo by manatou886 on Pixabay.com

Library and Archives Canada Cataloguing in Publication

Lin, Julia, 1962-, author
      Shadows of the crimson sun : one man's life in Manchuria, Taiwan, and North America / Julia Lin.

Includes bibliographical references.
Issued in print and electronic formats.
ISBN 978-1-988449-17-3 (softcover).—ISBN 978-1-988449-20-3 (HTML)

      1. Yang, Charles, 1932-. 2. Physicians—British Columbia—Vancouver—Biography. 3. Taiwanese Canadians—Biography. 4. Vancouver (B.C.)—Biography. I. Title.

FC3847.26.Y36L56 2017   971.1'3304092   C2017-904318-8
                                                        C2017-904319-6

Printed and bound in Canada by Coach House Printing

Mawenzi House Publishers Ltd.
39 Woburn Avenue (B)
Toronto, Ontario M5M 1K5
Canada
www.mawenzihouse.com

To the Yangs and other Taiwanese families
who braved the challenges of emigration

Contents

Charles at his Richmond home, 2016. Photo credit: Tracy Jean Wong.

Manchukuo (Japanese-controlled puppet state of Manchuria)

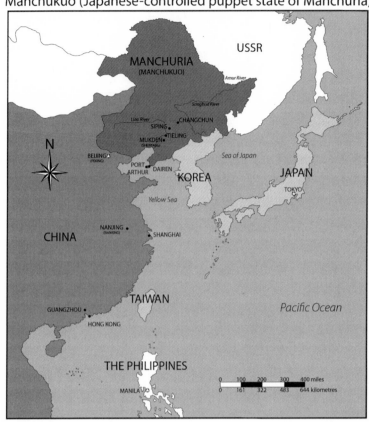

Taiwan

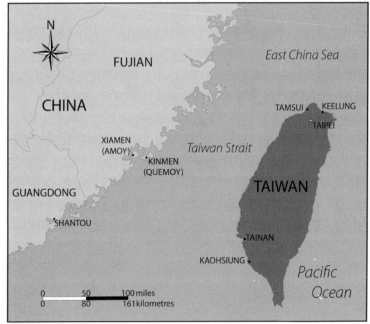

Prologue

As the bus travelled toward a downtown parking lot, he accepted the white cardboard mask from his seatmate and pressed it to his face. The stiff paper of the mask grated against his bearded chin and brushed against his spectacle lenses. The world before him blurred as he took off his thick glasses. His severe myopia had been both a curse and a blessing throughout his life; it had saved him from military service but it had also restricted his daily activities. Just once, he would have liked to wake up to a world in sharp focus.

Today, though, he was very clear in his purpose. His four-decade search for belonging was over. He was now firmly in one camp. His sojourns in Taiwan, Manchuria, America, and Canada had led him to this spot. His various identities, Akihisa Takayama, Masaaki Takayama, 楊正昭, Yang Cheng-Chao, C-C Yang, Charles Yang, were now inextricably fused into this one persona. No, not a persona, his true self.

The mask was crude and flimsy. Someone had cut out holes

for the eyes and mouth, but breathing would be difficult. Charles considered widening the mouth hole to reach his nose but there were no instruments at hand. It wasn't like in the operating room where he could have scissors passed to him on command. He sighed and put the elastic over his head then adjusted it to secure the mask. He was used to surgical masks, but he had never worn anything like this uncomfortable homemade one.

His father's admonitions against getting involved in politics reverberated dimly at the back of his mind. Charles believed the masks would offer protection. Besides, the cause was just. Everyone on this crowded bus of forty passengers felt the same way. But no one wanted to expose himself, man or woman. The risks were too great. Not only to themselves but also to their families and friends back in Taiwan. They had seen the consequences of defiance: jail, torture, and even murder by the government. Still, there was no other option. He lifted his glasses from his lap and hinged them over the mask.

Despite the seriousness of the cause, there was light-heartedness as well, camaraderie among friends. Their identities masked, they were safe to lodge their protests against injustice. Some of them were laughing and joking. Charles, too, felt safe behind his thin cardboard of a mask. But his sense of security would not hold. Before the day was done, he would put aside his mask and reveal himself publicly.

Part I

Manchuria
1934-1946
Akihisa Takayama

· 1 ·

Left Behind

MANCHURIA, 1940 – CITY OF FENGTIAN, 奉天 (JAPANESE: HŌTEN; ALSO MUKDEN; NOW SHENYANG, 瀋陽, IN CHINA)

Eight-year-old Akihisa Takayama stood at the doorway of his teacher's apartment building flanked by the middle-aged schoolmaster and his wife. Squinting in the glare of the bright midday sun, he watched the two rickshaws bearing his parents and three younger siblings away from him down the paved street of what travellers have described as the "painfully clean" Japanese section of the city, Yamato-ku.[1]

That morning, his father, Dr Takayama, had put on his three-piece suit and his mother her Western-style skirt and blouse. Amidst the flurry of last-minute packing, his mother had hurried Akihisa to dress. He had obediently donned a light shirt and short pants instead of his school uniform. He had even helped his younger brother, Tadahisa, find his good leather shoes. Finally the family completed their last preparations and hailed two rickshaws from among the pedicabs and carts, ubiquitous in the city, and delivered their eldest son to the schoolmaster.

Akihisa's world consisted only of his family and the Japanese community of Hōten. The other ethnic groups in the puppet state of Manchukuo played no role in his daily existence. His family rarely ventured out beyond the modern-looking streets and buildings of Yamato-ku to the squalor of the old Chinese section of town. Though his patients were later to be drawn from the five "races" of Manchukuo, at this time Akihisa's father, Dr Takayama, was employed as the physician of Yayoi Elementary School (彌生在滿小學校), where Akihisa was the only Japanese citizen of Taiwanese descent in attendance.[2] He had never known Manchuria by any name other than Manchukuo since he had been born after Japan renamed the region. Akihisa knew the meanings of the colours of the Manchukuo flag: red stripe representing bravery, blue stripe signifying justice, white stripe indicating purity, black stripe embodying determination, and the field of yellow representing unity. The five colours also represented the "races" of Manchuria: Chinese, Japanese, Manchus, Mongols, and Koreans. The same theme of racial harmony, *minzoku kyōwa*, was repeated in Manchukuo's stamps and postcards. Yet it was to Emperor Hirohito that Akihisa and his fellow students bowed each morning during *choukai*. It was to the Emperor that he wished *banzai*, "May he live ten thousand years," during morning assemblies. It was to Japan that he owed his allegiance.

Akihisa watched his family drawing away from him and a feeling of great loneliness descended upon him. It was the first time he had been away from home and the first time he had been without his family. He quickly brushed away the tears from his eyes, but the stream could not be stemmed. His father would have been ashamed of him. Akihisa was born on March 3, 1932, two days after the founding of Manchukuo, and had always striven to rise above the misfortune of being a boy born on Girls' Day. If he had to be born on a "day," why not on Boys' Day?[3] Not for him the dolls of

Girls' Day. Not for him the sniveling of the weaker sex. Boys were strong and brave. And they certainly never cried. That morning his father had reminded him that at the age of eight he himself had left home to board with a relative in Tainan in order to attend school. And here Akihisa's family was only going on vacation for a couple of months, and he was crying like a girl! Suddenly aware of the two adults beside him, Akihisa's embarrassment acted as the final spur for him to regain his composure.

"Come, Akihisa. Let us have some lunch, *neh?*" the kindly woman said.

Akihisa and the schoolmaster followed her through the hallway to their ground-floor apartment. She unlocked the door and led them down the corridor to the second of three rooms in the home. It was a six-tatami-mat room. Built from solid bricks and equipped with central heating to withstand cold Manchurian winters, the row of apartment buildings housed Japanese government employees and their dependents. Akihisa and his family lived in a similar building nearby.

As the schoolmaster's wife began to bring in the food and set the dishes on the low table, Akihisa sat patiently on his cushion beside the schoolmaster. Akihisa noticed that there was no girl to help her. At home, a Taiwanese girl had arrived a year ago to help his mother with the housework. The thought of his mother brought him close to tears again and he focused on sitting *seiza*-style on his cushion so his parents would not be ashamed of him. To show proper respect to his Japanese elders, Akihisa sat with his buttocks on his heels and his back straight. It was even more important for women to sit this way in order to preserve their modesty. His mother had told him the story of one woman who, aware that she was wearing no underwear beneath her underskirt as was customary, had refused to jump out of a burning building because of her fear of embarrassment and so had perished. (As an adult, Akihisa would recall this tale and think that, given traditionally liberal Japanese attitudes toward nudity, his mother had perhaps misunderstood the woman's motives or told the story through the lens of Chinese prudishness.)

To Akihisa's astonishment, after the schoolmaster's wife had set the meal on the table, she sat down with one knee flexed and the other leg extended under her kimono. He later found out that the woman suffered from an ailment in one knee that prevented her from flexing it without pain. At this meal, he merely marvelled at the informality of the Japanese at home, so different from their polite conduct at other times.

The schoolmaster's wife picked up her chopsticks and added *tonkatsu* (fried pork cutlet) and *takuan* (pickled daikon) to Akihisa's bowl of rice. She also ladled *misoshiru* into a bowl and set it in front of him. Akihisa lifted the bowl of soup to his mouth and took a sip. It did not taste like his mother's. Apparently, Japanese families made miso soup differently. He would rather have had another bowl of the congee that he'd had for breakfast instead of the fare in front of him. His mother's Taiwanese *muei* was not too thick or too watery and he loved the pickles and tofu that she always added. His late breakfast had also left him with little appetite for this early lunch, but Akihisa would not disgrace his family by being impolite, so he gamely downed the Japanese dishes.

"Akihisa, you will be with us for two months, so you will let me know if there is anything you need, *neh?*" said the schoolmaster's wife.

Akihisa nodded, but he knew that he would not complain about anything. His father had taught him the Taiwanese saying: Children have ears but no mouths. Akihisa was known for being *guai* ("obedient" in Taiwanese) and would be even more so in this unfamiliar Japanese home.

"Have you ever been to Taiwan, Akihisa?" the schoolmaster inquired.

Akihisa shook his head. He was born in Taiwan, but his parents then moved to Manchuria when he was two years old. His sister and youngest brother were both born in Manchuria. His father, then called Yang Jin Han (楊金涵), had graduated from Manchu Medical University in 1934 to join the corps of Taiwanese doctors active in Manchukuo.

The first Taiwanese physician arrived in Manchuria in 1905, when Japan gained control of Southern Manchuria at the end of the Russo-Japanese War. In the years between 1905 and 1945, over two hundred Taiwanese doctors were working in Manchuria. Of these, eighty-two, including Dr Takayama, as Dr Yang now called himself, had graduated from Manchu Medical University, while the rest had received their medical training in Taiwan, Japan, Korea, or other Manchurian institutions.[4] After graduation, Dr Takayama began working for the Ministry of Health, first in the Manchukuo capital of Shinkyō (新京),[5] and now in Hōten.

Taiwan had been made a Japanese colony in 1895, according to the Treaty of Shimonoseki, which concluded the First Sino-Japanese War and made Japan the first modern Asian imperialist power. The Japanese were determined to carry out modern reforms in this formerly neglected and backward Chinese territory. Under Japanese rule, great improvements had been made in Taiwan's infrastructure, economy, education, and health system. However, the native Taiwanese were not given genuine political powers. Dr Takayama had initially studied law at Meiji University in Tokyo but soon realized there was no future for a Taiwanese in that field. For young men of ability, the most common profession was medicine, a choice encouraged by the Japanese government.

Ironically, it was these doctors trained in the Japanese system who agitated for political reform during the 1920s. Always treated as second-class citizens in their own land, they now demanded a political voice. But this movement began to decline through the 1930s, and especially after *kōminka*, an intense Japanization program, was introduced in 1937. Implemented after the outbreak of the Second Sino-Japanese War, *kōminka* sought to "erase the Han Chinese identity of the Taiwanese people and to enhance the loyalty of the Taiwanese to the mother country."[6] The program succeeded to some degree in three of its objectives: language acquisition, name changes, and military recruitment, but it was unsuccessful in eradicating native customs in religion and social practices. By 1945, records show that more than 80% of the Taiwanese were fluent in Japanese and about 7% had adopted Japanese names.[7] Leading the wave of assimilation were the physicians who saw Japanese practices as progressive. These former leaders of anticolonial protests were thus the first to adopt the ways of their colonizers.[8]

Even with Japan's attempt to assimilate them, the Taiwanese saw their prospects in Taiwan as limited due to their ethnicity. With the addition of Manchukuo to Japan's "Great Empire," young Taiwanese found a land of greater opportunity. The Japanese government even established the tuition-free Kenkoku University in 1938 and actively recruited Taiwanese students to fill its ethnic quotas. The university's stated mission was to promote racial harmony: the five "races" as well as the Taiwanese and the Russians were represented in this short-lived Manchukuo integration endeavour.

Throughout the 1930s, adventurous Taiwanese students, civil servants, and physicians migrated to this frontier land to try their luck. As Japanese subjects in a Japanese protectorate, the Taiwanese in Manchuria were able to live openly as Taiwanese instead of hiding their identities like those in other parts of China who feared being mistaken for Japanese enemies.[9] About 5,000 Taiwanese doctors, teachers, engineers and technicians, many of whom worked for the South Manchurian Railway Company, made their homes in Manchuria between 1931 and 1945.[10] Dr Yang was one of these pioneers.

Like many elite Taiwanese of the time, Dr Yang had adopted a Japanese last name, Takayama (高山, high mountain). But even the enthusiastic supporters of modernization retained a deep loyalty to their island of origin. The Yangs chose their new name as a tribute to the highest mountain in Taiwan, Yushan or Jade Mountain, which had been renamed Niitakayama (新高山, new high mountain) by the Japanese. Known in the West as Mount Morrison, after the American freighter captain who first sighted the mountain in the nineteenth century, the peak was even higher than Mount Fuji. Niitakayama would later become notorious as part of the coded message to Japanese naval troops that began the attack on Pearl Harbor: Climb the Niitakayama.[11] For Dr Yang, Takayama was likely an indication of his optimism for the future and his hopes for his young family.

In a nod to the Chinese tradition of choosing auspicious names based on the number of strokes in the three characters comprising first and last names, Dr Yang had chosen the family's new Japanese names by counting character strokes. Despite the fact that four of them already had Chinese names, he felt the need to start anew. In a twist on the Chinese tradition, Dr Takayama renamed each member of the family by choosing kanji with eight strokes for the first character and three strokes for the second character in the belief that the names would bring them good luck.[12]

It was difficult at first for Akihisa to answer to his Japanese name at school because his mother still called him Masaaki at home. When the four children became adults, they would all cast off their Japanese names. Asked what his Japanese name was, 正昭 would give the Japanese pronunciation of his Chinese name, Masaaki, instead of Akihisa.

From his earliest years, Akihisa's parents had spoken mostly Japanese with him and he felt he was Japanese. His family held Japanese passports and they enjoyed almost the same privileges as the Japanese. Although his parents spoke Taiwanese with each other, Akihisa knew only a smattering of his mother tongue. His family observed all the Japanese festivals and only a few of the Chinese ones. The celebration they'd had for *Shichi-Go-San* (七五三)[13] on November 15 was one of the most memorable. He watched enviously as his three-year-old sister and his five-year-old brother were given the same number of *chitose ame* (thousand-year candy) as their ages. The red and white candies came inside paper bags decorated with cranes and turtles, which symbolized longevity. His sister would now be allowed to grow her hair long and his brother would be able to wear a *hakama* like the men.

For Akihisa, Taiwan was an abstract idea and he had no strong affection for it. He knew that it never snowed there. That held some attraction, since the bitter Manchurian winters often left him frostbitten. He only regretted being separated from his family during these weeks while he was in the midst of the first term of school. The Japanese school year began in April and the sole reason Akihisa had been left behind was because his father felt he could not afford to miss any part of the first trimester. Dr Takayama valued academics above all.

The rest of the midday meal proceeded uneventfully and Akihisa did nothing to bring shame to himself. At the conclusion of lunch the schoolmaster said, "Well, you'll be back in school tomorrow. In the meantime, you can review your homework."

Akihisa enjoyed school. He liked his school uniform, which consisted of a hat with a visor, a green jacket with gold-coloured buttons, and matching short pants. He had always performed well enough to be consistently named class monitor, an honour given to the top academic student each term. He took the responsibility seriously. He diligently kept the students in order when the teacher had to leave the classroom. On the rare occasions when money had to be collected (tuition was free in Japanese-run schools), he carefully accounted for all tenders. And he never failed to call out "Stand up!" loudly when the teacher entered the room, and then they all bowed low to show respect to the schoolmaster. It felt strange to be in the home of a *sensei* and see him crunch his food and pick his teeth.

It would be even stranger to walk to school with this man. Even though his parents were protective, Akihisa had been allowed to walk to school on his own ever since he started Grade One. Yamato-ku held few hazards for children and Akihisa never felt threatened. His parents had given him strict instructions not to stray from his daily route and he did not dally despite the temptations of the bookshops, toy stores, and grocery storefronts.

The only part of school that Akihisa was less than enthusiastic about was physical education. He was not a fast runner, therefore soccer was a struggle. The parallel and single bars in gymnastics were an ordeal since he could not do a proper chin-up. Even baseball was not fun. Since his father's mantra of "study, study, study" dominated all his instructions to his son about school, Akihisa had been little bothered by his lack of athletic prowess. Had his father encouraged him to excel in sports, Akihisa would doubtless have exerted himself more. His father's word was law to the young boy and Akihisa continued in the Confucian tradition of complete obedience to the head of the household. As it was, he rushed to study whenever his father was near for he wished to please him and even the pleasure of reading 少年クラブ, the Shonen Club monthly children's magazines, was limited to hours when his homework had been completed. He wished he had brought some copies of the magazine to the teacher's house so he could read the mangas. Even the patriotic stories would do right now. But homework first.

That night, after the evening meal had been cleared and the tables and cushions moved aside, Akihisa found himself sharing the same room with the schoolmaster's brother. He stared as the young man slid open the *shōji* and stepped onto the tatami. He continued slack-jawed as the man took a futon, duvet, and pillows out of the storage closet. Akihisa's fascination was not with what the man was doing, because his mother also stored the family bedding in *oshiire* and the multipurpose eating area at home also converted to a bedroom at night, but with the man's attire. It was the first time Akihisa had ever seen anyone in a *fundoshi*. He had seen his father in undershirt and shorts before but never in a loincloth like this. He had thought only sumo wrestlers sported such apparel. How funny to see it on an ordinary person!

As he stretched out timidly beside the man, Akihisa realized how different he was from the Japanese. Even though he spoke perfect Japanese, lived in the Japanese part of town, and his schoolmasters taught him that he was a full Japanese citizen, Akihisa knew he was not the same as the *naichijin* (an insider); he would always be a *gaichijin* (outsider) like the Koreans and the other Taiwanese. Though he had never experienced ill treatment by his schoolmasters, some part of him had always known he was not a real Japanese, much as he wished he were. His mother did not wear kimonos to parent-teacher conferences like the other mothers. His parents spoke Taiwanese with each other. The family photo album contained pictures of grandparents in embroidered robes standing in front of wooden Chinese buildings. Even the food they ate was different. Though his school lunches, like those of other students, were sometimes *Hinomaru bentos* with white rice and a single red *umeboshi* (red salted plum) lodged in the middle to represent the Japanese flag, he suspected his classmates did not eat congee for lunch at home.

He recalled a playground incident. Because the Japanese settlers in Manchuria originated from different parts of Japan, it was not uncommon for Japanese schoolboys to ask their fellows where they came from, meaning from what specific region of Japan their families emigrated. When his turn came, instead of admitting the truth, Akihisa had instantly named a place in Japan. He knew the Japanese regarded honesty as a top virtue but the lie had slipped out. How he wished he were a true Japanese!

Although Akihisa perceived no discrimination personally while in Manchuria, he would discover decades later that despite being at the top of his class he had been sent by his Japanese teachers to a second-tier middle school instead of the first-ranked school in Hōten. He would also find out that the Taiwanese had initially been given food rations similar to those allotted to Koreans and allowances had only been increased to Japanese levels after some of the Taiwanese protested.

Young Akihisa was oblivious to the treatment of the Japanese toward *gaichijin*. He only knew his aloneness. He missed his mother Shuko's songs. Trained in Taiwan as an elementary school teacher, his mother had worked to help support her husband's education, a fact that she frequently mentioned to her children. Naturally her training only allowed her to teach Taiwanese children. Later, when the lines between the Taiwanese and the Japanese were blurred under the *kōminka* reforms, her prospects improved, but then she was already in Manchuria raising her young family. She never taught school again.

Shuko's knowledge of Japanese songs was vast. She had taught her children tunes such as "Tsuki" (The Moon), "Yuki" (Snow), "Kisha" (The Train), and "Shabon Dama" (Bubbles) even before Akihisa started school. There was also a lesser-known one about four-leaf clovers that she liked to sing. She believed that finding one meant good luck, and she was always on the lookout for four-leaf clovers wherever she went.

She often told the story of a singing competition in which she sang a melancholic song about her parental home but was so overcome with emotion near the end that she was unable to continue. The adjudicators were so impressed with the sincerity of her delivery that they awarded her first prize. The song, "Kokyo no Sora" (Under the Sky of My Homeland), went

Yuuzora harete akikaze fuki
Tsuki-kage ochite suzumushi naku
Omoeba tooshi kokyou no sora
Ah, ah, waga chichi-haha ika ni owasu . . .

(Clear evening sky and autumn breeze blowing
Moon shadow on the ground and bell crickets singing
I think, how far is the sky of my homeland
Ah, ah, I wonder how my father and my mother are faring . . .)

He hummed it in his head because he didn't want to disturb the man sleeping next to him. Then he thought of another song that his mother had taught him, called "Ame Furi" (Falling Rain): *Ame ame fure fure kaasan ga, Ja nome de omukai ureshiina . . .* (Rain, rain falling from the sky, My mother will come with her umbrella..). He could almost hear his mother calling to him, *Masa-chan . . .*

Tears threatened to fall again but this time Akihisa controlled himself like a Japanese samurai. Despite the differences between *naichijin* and *gaichijin*, here in Manchuria, he aspired to be as good a Japanese as he could be. His purpose in life was to serve Emperor and country to the best of his ability, just as his schoolmasters had taught him. His parents had brought him to this land where there were no limits to what he could achieve and he was determined not to disappoint them.

· 2 ·

Field Study

Akihisa wiped the sweat off his brows with a handkerchief and took a sip of water from his canteen. Even though it was only midmorning, the summer heat was already unbearable. He gazed up at 203-Metre Hill and resigned himself to the trek up one of the most important battle sites in the Russo-Japanese War. He would never have been a good soldier in that conflict. The thought of making a bayonet charge up the hill on a freezing December night while hand grenades and machine gun fire rained down from above sickened him. He shuddered when he imagined the thousands of soldiers who had died gloriously for the Emperor in 1904. Layers of dead bodies piled on top of each other, some in the valley below, some wedged in the barbed wire entanglements that the Russians had erected as barriers, others closer to the Russian fortifications at the summit.[1] He knew he would not have had the courage to refuse orders but at the same time he didn't know if he would have had the courage to obey them either. He was glad he was only eleven and not old enough to serve in the current war.

As it was, he would have to follow the teacher's command and scale this wretchedly steep hill. At least the schoolmaster, a young man, had released them from troop formation; they had been marching three abreast, like the soldiers would have done while on parade. Their khaki school uniforms were modelled after those of the soldiers, and their conduct copied from army discipline. Even their canteens were oval, metallic, and covered with cloth like those of real soldiers.

In the 1910s and 1920s, some Japanese educators had favoured the "New Education Movement"[2] fashioned after the ideas of John Dewey, but by the start of the Second Sino-Japanese War in 1937, extreme nationalists ruled the country and the school curricula reflected the change.[3] Elementary school teacher manuals mirrored the ultranationalist Shinto bent of the government. Sixty-five percent of school lessons contained war propaganda and served the state agenda.[4] Students were taught how to bow to the Imperial portraits, how to worship the Shinto goddess Amaterasu, and when to fly the national flag at home.[5] Like the schoolchildren in Japan proper, Manchurian students visited Shinto shrines and war memorials regularly. The eighth day of each month was devoted to lessons about the war.

All the boys in Akihisa's class aspired to be generals or admirals when they grew up.

Despite being steeped in militarism at school, Akihisa did not desire to serve the Emperor in that way. Even though he played war games with his younger brothers and sister at home, his natural distaste for violence prohibited him from wanting to be a soldier. But a sense of shame at his cowardice prevented him from voicing his true feelings. Nevertheless, he earnestly believed that Japan was fighting a holy war to free Asia from Western imperialists. His schoolmasters taught him that Japan's enemies, the British and the Americans, were devils who would kill or rape at any opportunity. Their grab for land in the East had subjected Orientals to great hardships. But now they were paying for their greed. Supplies of coal in England had been depleted and British policemen could not stop the looters roaming the streets. In America, factories were being sabotaged and major cities terrorized by race riots. On the Chinese mainland, it was the duty of the superior Japanese race to save the Chinese from the Westerners who had humiliated them for so long. The Japanese would rescue the homeless and starving Chinese who were hiding in caves throughout China.[6]

According to the teachers it was "Japan's destiny to bring Asia into the modern era."[7] Asians were tired of being bullied by the West. Why was it that the Washington Naval Treaty limited Japan to building three tons of battleships and aircraft carriers for every five that Britain and the United States were allowed? What gave foreign devils the right to colonize Orientals? Japan was the protector of Asia. British Malaya, Singapore, Hong Kong, Dutch East Indies, and the Philippines had already been liberated.

For Akihisa, accounts of the war were unreal stories from distant lands. Ever since he was five, with the start of the Second Sino-Japanese War, he had known warfare as a way of life. But he had not seen any fighting in Manchuria and he was living contentedly. To his knowledge, his family had not experienced significant deprivations, nor had their neighbours. Though food was rationed, there was always plenty to eat. He did not know that at the Manchu Medical University, his father's alma mater, Chinese students ate kaoliang (Chinese sorghum) while the Japanese students ate white rice. That it became illegal for all Chinese to eat rice as the war progressed.[8] Nor did he know that in his parents' homeland the Japanese were given "A" rations while the Taiwanese were given "C" rations and only Taiwanese with family members serving in the Japanese military or favoured by Japanese officials were given "B" rations. Since he had little contact with the locals, Akihisa perceived no injustice in the treatment of the Japanese toward the rest of the people of Manchuria. It was just the way things were. He did not question the functioning of his world.

Nor did he ever question his teachers' orders. With some misgivings, Akihisa stepped away from the other boys and began the hike up the hill. Though their school was co-ed, there were only boys on this field trip. Accompanied by five teachers and a number of older students, the group of ninety schoolboys was under tight control. Akihisa and other students in Grade Five had been organized into a troop under the care of Mr Saito, a smart and handsome man whom Akihisa admired even though he had never been in his class. Like other teachers, Mr Saito was in Western dress. As Akihisa stopped to pull up his white knee socks and pull his sweat-stained school uniform away from his back, he wondered how Mr Saito could look so cool in his three-piece suit.

The schoolmaster glanced at Akihisa as he strayed from the group but allowed him to journey alone. Akihisa was surprised and grateful. He had had enough of these boys. An introvert by nature, Akihisa did not have a close friend at school. Instead, he was quietly accepted as he floated from group to group but never formed the nucleus of any one clique. His best friends were his younger siblings.

Perhaps, deep down, caution and a sense of inferiority prevented him from getting too close to the Japanese boys. He did not want them to discover his Taiwanese background. He would be subject to bullying if he were found to be different. The Japanese stressed conformity. Differences were to be avoided at all costs. He considered himself lucky not to be targeted for his scholastic ability, since Japanese boys prized athletics over academics. Then too there was the deference to authority and the distinctions in ranks. He had seen younger boys slapped or pinched on the street for not saluting boys only one grade above them. The older a boy got, the more pronounced the hierarchical orders and the more severe the penalties for disregarding them. Much as he liked school, Akihisa loathed the social norms that prevailed.

Given Akihisa's dislike of physical activity, the steep climb was unpleasant. The path was wide and, as eleven-year-old boys will, some of his classmates roughhoused. They threw up dust and chased each other, some even straying off the path to run around the evergreen trees, which were planted after 1905 by Japanese settlers, when the hill was barren. This had been termed by newspapers as a "liberal legacy for future generations"; Japan was setting an example for the world.[9] Akihisa was proud to belong to such a forward-thinking nation.

As he trudged up the hill, Akihisa kept his eye out for artefacts from the war, small though the chances were of finding them now. Soon after the war, and even as late as 1909, visitors would find brass shells and casings and even human bones and teeth.[10] The hill had become a picnic spot for Japanese tourists eager to find souvenirs, evidence of Japan's military strength.[11] As expected, Akihisa found nothing, but he knew he would be able to buy all sorts of souvenirs from the stores in Port Arthur.[12] Then he remembered his parents would regard such purchases as wasteful, so he quashed any thoughts of assuaging his disappointment this way.

Even so, the field study trip had been exciting. It was his first school trip away from home, and his mother had fussed before his departure, remembering little things that he might need even up to the moment he left the house. A special snack, another pencil, more clean underwear, a bit of extra spending money—all accompanied by yet another reminder to be careful and to obey the teachers. She had wanted to see him off at the train station but her duties at home had prevented her. Instead, his father had left his clinic unattended and engaged a rickshaw to drop Akihisa and his luggage off at school.

After his family's return from their Taiwanese vacation three years ago, Dr Takayama had transferred to a small town called Tetsurei, sixty kilometres north of Hōten. Later he left the Ministry of Health entirely and started his own practice. Dr Takayama drew many of his patients from the mostly Japanese, Chinese, and Manchurian employees of the South Manchurian Railway Company (SMRC). He ran a walk-in clinic at his home and also paid house calls. His association with the Company helped his practice immensely. *Mantetsu* was easily the largest employer in Manchuria, with more than two hundred thousand workers.[13]

The SMRC was more than just a railway company. The first president of the SMRC, Gotō Shimpei, former Japanese governor of Taiwan, saw it as an instrument of colonial control. Its avowed mission in 1906 was *bunsō teki bubi*, "military preparedness in civil garb," which meant "invasion in civilian disguise."[14] Gotō aimed to win over the Manchurians through providing modern facilities.[15] The SMRC built schools, hospitals, libraries, and sanitation plants. The medical college from which Dr Takayama had graduated was established by the SMRC for the purpose initially of training Chinese doctors. The SMRC also constructed research facilities, such as the Geological Research Institute, the Central Laboratory, and several agricultural experimental stations.[16]

Gotō envisioned bringing in 500,000 Japanese settlers to solidify the Japanization of Manchuria.[17] It was not until after the founding of Manchukuo, when the Japanese Kantō Army was in full control and each Manchurian government official had a Japanese "advisor" or deputy minister that massive immigration began. Between 1932 and 1945, an estimated 300,000 Japanese settlers arrived in Manchuria under the Village Division Campaign.[18] These Japanese colonists and the rest of the more than two million Japanese on the Chinese mainland[19] were transported across Manchuria by 15,000 kilometres of rail, most of which was laid down by the SMRC in this "rural utopia."[20]

Accustomed to the local railways, Akihisa was awed by his first sight of the Asia Express, pride of the South Manchurian Railway, as they boarded in Hōten. The sleek, enclosed locomotive was beautiful, so unlike the dirty, old-fashioned smoke-stacked local engines. The carriages looked new and modern; once the train got underway, even the rowdiest boys were hushed by the rate of travel. Capable of a top speed of over 130 kilometres per hour, the Asia Express was the fastest train in Asia and, Akihisa believed, of the world. Expanses of cultivated fields and broad plains interspersed with occasional towns, dams, and mountains sped by. Akihisa conscientiously noted down sightings of battlefields from the Russo-Japanese War as the teachers pointed them out. The nearly 400 kilometres from Hōten to Dairen were covered in less than five hours.

He was as awed by Dairen when they arrived in the busy city. In 1898, when the Russians took control of *Dal'nii*,[21] Tsar Nicholas II had intended to develop the obscure Chinese fishing village into the "Paris of the East." Conceived as a city of parks and well-connected promenades patterned after Paris, the city was to cover eighty hectares.[22] But before the plan could be completed, the Japanese had driven the Russians out.

Like many Japanese, Akihisa saw the Russian presence in Dairen as another example of Western imperialism, and the Russian defeat in 1905 as the righting of an injustice. The Russians had been particularly odious in their quest for an ice-free port just before the turn of the century. Akihisa had been taught about the terms of the Treaty of Shimonoseki that ended the 1895 Sino-Japanese War. Under the treaty, Japan acquired Taiwan and part of the Liaodong Peninsula, including Dairen and Port Arthur. Within a week, Russia, France and Germany had intervened and the three powers "advised" retrocession; war-weakened Japan was forced to give up the Peninsula. A few months after the Triple Intervention, the Russians extracted a lease agreement from China that gave them control over the land that Japan had just returned.

The Japanese were understandably enraged. So it was with great satisfaction that Japan took back the Peninsula, including the supposedly impregnable Russian fortification of Port Arthur, in the Russo-Japanese War. Thus Japan became the first Asian country to defeat a Western state. The victory was especially impressive given the size of Russia's armed forces.

Akihisa swelled with pride when he was taught of Japan's glorious achievement. He thought the Russians deserved defeat especially for their ignoble handling of the Port Arthur affair with respect to the Chinese. After the First Sino-Japanese War, Russia had signed a treaty with China promising protection in the event of a Japanese attack. As the lone dissenting voice in the Russian government, Finance Minister Sergei Witte, allegedly said: "To break an agreement so soon after signing it, and worse, to behave like a brigand after swearing to be China's protector, was faithless and despicable."[23] Thus were sown the seeds of Akihisa's life-long bias against Russians.

In comparison with the aborted Russian plans for Dairen, Japanese development of the port city was impressive. To accommodate the rapidly growing population, blueprints soon ballooned to detail a harbour of six wharves and a city of 2000 hectares.[24] At the centre of the city was Oh-hiro-ba Park with a bronze statue of General Ohshima, the first governor of Kantō-shu.[25] The Japanese had continued the Russian theme and kept the Parisian Place de l'Étoile layout.[26] Streets named after military heroes of the Russo-Japanese War formed the arms of the city's starlike layout.[27] Imposing Western-style buildings, including the British Embassy, the Japanese government building, the major banks, and the Yamato Hotel surrounded the park.[28]

The Yamato Hotel edifice was truly magnificent. The five-storey building had a majestic staircase, hallways carpeted in red, gold mouldings, and pink marble walls. Built in 1909, it was proof of Japan's "civilizing" influence in Manchuria.[29] But all the Yamato Hotels admitted only Japanese guests.

Akihisa's school group had been housed at another Yamato Hotel when they arrived in Ryojun (Port Arthur), albeit one not as grand as the building in Dairen. After almost a week, the novelty of being with his classmates had worn off, and Akihisa wished they would be less boisterous. The boys had been slow to settle most nights and Akihisa was suffering the effects of sleep deprivation. Boys played marbles, from which pillow fights and fistfights ensued. There was interminable poking and shoving when the teacher wasn't looking. He would much rather have been at home in the room that he shared with his brother, instead of playing tourist.

Akihisa was accustomed to seeing busloads of tourists from Japan proper in the streets of Hōten. Since Chinese history was not taught in Japanese schools, Akihisa knew little about the city's past. His father had told him that Hōten was the former Manchu capital, and the ancient mausoleums where the Manchu emperors were buried were located in the north and east of the city. The Battle of Mukden had been the decisive conflict in the Russo-Japanese War and most tourists came to visit the victory memorials and the Manchurian tombs.[30] Mukden was also the site of the 1931 incident that led to the Japanese occupation of Manchuria but Akihisa did not think there was a memorial for that. Manchuria had seen a leap in tourism in 1940 when Japan celebrated the 2600th anniversary of the founding of the Imperial dynasty. Even now, in the thick of war, despite Empire-wide campaigns encouraging frugality, travel was still officially sanctioned.[31] Tours to "sacred sites" in Japan and the colonies increased patriotic fervour. Outside of Japan proper, Port Arthur was the most popular tourist destination for the Japanese.[32] Visits to war memorials and battlefields were an integral part of Akihisa's education.

Akihisa let out a sigh of relief, catching his breath, when he finally reached the summit. He craned his neck and gazed up at the war memorial constructed to resemble a bomb. It looked like a gigantic, upright bullet. Squeezing through the crowd of boys to read the inscription, he recognized the famous poem of General Nogi, who led the attacks on 203-Metre Hill.[33] If forced to serve, Akihisa thought he would aspire to be like Nogi, a poet-soldier. A man who believed in the justness of his cause; whose nobility of character prevented him from sparing his second son's participation in the final battle, despite having lost his first son earlier. He ended up without an heir. His obedience to the Emperor's command was the only deterrent to committing suicide due to his sense of shame and failure at the enormous number of casualties suffered under his command.

But Akihisa was certain he did not have the makings of a good soldier, let alone a celebrated scholar-samurai. He scanned the groups of boys milling around the memorial and wondered if any of them had what it took. His classmates could all expect to go to college and then embark on careers as respectable middle-class professionals or businessmen. Everyone expected the war to end quickly. After all, Japan had begun the war with such spectacular victories. The chances that Akihisa and his classmates would be pressed into service were slim.

Mr Saito posed the class for a picture next to the 217 kg howitzer used in in the war.[34] More than 11,000 cannonballs had been fired in the final battles, enough to destroy the Russian Pacific fleet anchored in the harbour and ensure Japanese victory during the Battle of Tsushima, Mr Saito said. Think about the sacrifices they made so you can stand here today, class. He then led the boys in singing *heitai-san yo arigato* (Thank you, Soldiers). Akihisa sang it with heartfelt conviction.

Decades later, Akihisa would remember these lessons, even after recollections of the trip's particulars had dimmed and he would have to fill in the gaps the best he could. Especially vivid were details regarding the 1905 Battle of Tsushima. Just before the battle began, Admiral Tōgō had signaled his men: "The fate of the Empire depends on this battle. Let every man do his utmost." This victory against an enemy that outnumbered them became the most celebrated in Japanese naval history, the equivalent of the Battle of Trafalgar for the British.[35] Akihisa would be fond of pointing out that Nelson had signaled the same sentiment exactly a hundred years earlier when he faced the numerically superior French and Spanish fleets. He would delight in the parallels between the decisive battles that had changed the courses of the Napoleonic and the Russo-Japanese wars. Seventy years after that field study, Akihisa's pride in Japanese accomplishments would remain intact.

When the students were allowed to disperse, Akihisa made his way to the low ramparts and looked out over Port Arthur. The entire city was spread out below in front of him. How narrow and small the harbour seemed! It was a sight to remember. The song to the soldiers still rang in his ears. He had no doubt they would protect him. Although he feared military service, he would do his duty if required. But he was certain he would not be pressed into service given the strength of the nation. He did not know that Japan had already lost the decisive Battle of Midway the year before, and the tide had turned against them in the Pacific War. In two short years, his sense of security would be completely shattered, and his life as a privileged Japanese citizen would be over.

Encounter at Gunpoint

TETSUREI (MODERN-DAY TIELING, 鐵嶺, CHINA), 1945

If the knock had come in the evening, they would not have opened the door. To his recollection, it was the first time Akihisa had ever seen his father make an error. Akihisa had always relied on his father's good judgment. Right in the middle of the rainy season in August, the Russians had invaded Manchuria. News of the surprise attacks reached Hōten, where thirteen-year-old Akihisa was boarding with his schoolmaster's wife and aged mother, while attending middle school. Like many Japanese men, the schoolmaster was now serving in the armed forces. Holed up for several days with the two women in the apartment, awaiting news from his family, Akihisa was immensely relieved to see his twenty-year-old cousin, Yu-san Lin, appear. He greeted Yu-san with a heartfelt *arigato* and hurried to pack his bags.

Throughout Asia, it was common for doctors to fill prescriptions on site. Many patients did not feel that they had been properly treated unless they walked away with medicines. Dr Takayama's medical practice had grown to the point where he was able to sponsor his wife's nephew from Taiwan to act as his pharmacy assistant. Yu-san had arrived in Hōten after a ten-day sea voyage, the ship from Keelung to Dairen having had to take refuge in the Chinese port of Qingdao for several days to dodge American submarines. Following the attack on Pearl Harbor in 1941, the United States had entered the war in the Pacific and the waters between Taiwan and Manchuria had become treacherous with Allied ships and submarines. But it was not until August 9, 1945 that the Second World War was fought on Manchurian soil and the Takayamas experienced the war firsthand.

The Japanese in Manchuria had believed they were safe from Russian invasion because of the five-year Neutrality Pact between Japan and the USSR. The pact was to expire in 1946, but in April 1945 the Soviets gave Japan notice that it would not be renewed; worse, the Russians had already made a secret agreement with the United States and Britain at the Yalta Conference in February, promising to attack Japan within three months of Germany's surrender. Accordingly, Stalin gave orders to start moving troops to the Soviet-Manchurian border soon after Germany's defeat.

On August 8, 1945, exactly three months after Germany's unconditional surrender, the USSR declared war on Japan. A well-planned pincer attack to the east and west of Manchuria began the following day as forces previously amassed at the borders were unleashed.[1] Caught off-guard and confused by conflicting orders (some Japanese soldiers thought they were to surrender while others refused to believe the orders or had not received any), the outnumbered and outgunned Japanese were overpowered by the invading tank columns. With troops numbering 1.8 million versus the Japanese Kantō (Kwantung) Army's seven hundred thousand,[2] the Russians made rapid progress across the vast stretches of Manchuria to reach the cities in the heartland within a few weeks. Akihisa would hold what he saw as Russian treachery tight in his heart throughout his life.

Dr Takayama dispatched Yu-san to bring Akihisa home from Hōten as soon as news of the invasion reached him. By then, the trains had stopped running. Fortunately, one of Dr Takayama's patients was the Tetsurei stationmaster's wife. The stationmaster arranged for a locomotive to be sent to Hōten at the earliest opportunity. Staffed only by an engineer and a fireman, the steam locomotive made the forty-minute trip from Tetsurei early the next morning. On the return trip, Yu-san and Akihisa were obliged to ride inside the tender atop the coal supply, there being no passenger cars attached to the locomotive. Akihisa found the ride thrilling despite being covered with soot and choked by billowing black smoke as they chugged home. That train ride was one of Akihisa's most memorable experiences in Manchuria.

Upon arrival in Tetsurei, the soot-darkened pair engaged a rickshaw to take them home, riding past predominantly Japanese-owned businesses that had closed their doors since the chaos began: hotels, ice cream shops, banks, pharmacies, barber shops, sporting goods stores, printing shops, and the local movie theatre. Even the Chinese watch store was closed.

Weeks of uncertainty followed, with little official news. Not knowing what to expect, Dr Takayama kept his family indoors. The first time that the Takayamas realized that the war was lost was when Emperor Hirohito made his radio address declaring unconditional surrender on August 15. Despite the crackling reception and frustrating moments of utter silence, they were able to gather the gist of the message. A wordless disbelief fell upon the family. Even the normally authoritative and opinionated doctor had nothing to say on the subject. He joined the rest of the citizens of the Japanese Empire in their bewilderment. Weeping women and disillusioned men who had believed in the might of the Asian military powerhouse were tossed into an abyss of crushing uncertainty and powerlessness. Their government had collapsed and the Japanese in Manchuria were left stranded in a hostile land. For many, their subsequent struggle for survival would end in death.

They had been taught to believe that Japan could not lose the war. After all, the Shinto gods had protected the Imperial dynasty from foreign conquest for more than twenty-six hundred years. They still remembered that the Kamikaze, the divine wind sent by the gods, had twice stymied the invasion of Japan by the Mongols in the thirteenth century by destroying their ships in typhoons. Surely the Sun Goddess Amaterasu would not allow a nation ruled by her direct descendant, Emperor Hirohito, to come to harm. After nearly fifteen years of fighting, from the Manchurian Incident[3] of 1931 to the present, how was it possible that all the sacrifices had been for naught? They had been exhorted to fight to the death in the name of the Emperor, to defend Japan's home islands to the last. Given the choice between surrender, let alone *unconditional* surrender, and death, it was more honourable to choose death.

It was a measure of the success of government propaganda and total belief in the Emperor's divinity that so many Japanese refused to accept the final outcome or, if they did, took drastic measures in keeping with their ideals. For instance, on the island of Saipan, thousands of Japanese civilians opted for or were coerced into jumping off cliffs in acts of mass suicide rather than face capture by the victorious Americans.[4] These acts of devotion to the Emperor manage to astonish even modern Japanese citizens.

News about the war had been carefully filtered and disseminated by the propaganda machine at the Daihonei Hōdōbu, the Imperial General Headquarters. *Shisōsen*, the "thought war," was considered an essential part of the war effort.[5] In the early years of World War II, when Japan was making rapid conquests throughout Southeast Asia, radios, newspapers, films, and public loudspeakers spread the good news. As Japan began to lose ground in the latter part of the war, the Daihonei kept citizens in the dark about the setbacks. Retreats were described as "lateral advancements;" stories about heroic *kamikaze* soldiers were played up; the atomic bombings of Hiroshima and Nagasaki were euphemized as resulting from a "new kind of bomb" that caused more damage than usual. Akihisa would later dismiss the propaganda as politicians and bureaucrats flagrantly "playing with words."

Though some Japanese began to realize the futility of continued fighting, for the most part, they dared not voice their opinions for fear of being accused of thought crimes. It was a serious offense to doubt government proclamations, let alone to stand up against government positions. Ironically, for the Taiwanese who eventually returned to their home island, these Japanese government prohibitions were to be recalled as mild in comparison with the restrictions under which they found themselves after the Chinese Kuomintang government took over Taiwan.

By August 21, Soviet troops had "liberated" Hōten and other major cities in Manchuria. Months of terror ensued. Russian commanders did little to rein in the conduct of their troops. It was apparently the custom for Soviet officers to allow their soldiers indulgence in the spoils of war during the first few days after conquest. But in Manchuria, the madness lasted much longer. While the Japanese were primarily targeted, the rest of the Manchurian population also suffered. The Russians were feared and hated by both the Chinese and the Japanese. "Big nose no good" was a common Chinese remark when speaking of the Soviets long after their departure.[6]

Soviet soldiers were seen as thuggish and uncouth. There were reports of soldiers pulling drivers in their own rickshaws for novelty, and of infantrymen scattering bank notes for local citizens to retrieve.[7] The Russians apparently had not seen many of the amenities of a modern Japanese city, such as light bulbs and water taps. There were many instances of theft.[8] Japanese houses were often emptied of furniture before soldiers set fire to them.[9]

The Soviet government ordered the systematic dismantling of Japanese industrial equipment almost as soon as the troops arrived. Making use of Manchuria's natural resources, the Japanese had made Manchukuo into an industrial dynamo. Between 1932 and 1941, the Japanese had invested an estimated 5.9 billion yen in Manchuria.[10] Besides the South Manchurian Railway Company, there was also mining and manufacturing. Heavy industry manufactured tools, aircraft, trucks, munitions, construction and farm equipment, and factories produced consumer goods such as textiles, boots, carpets, rubber products, and paper. Equipment from public buildings, including hospitals and laboratories, were loaded onto railway cars and shipped to Siberia. Modern tools were prized while older equipment was either destroyed or left behind for Chinese looters. The 1946 report of Edwin Pauley, US Commissioner of Reparations, put the total cost of replacement due to destruction, removal, and deterioration at two billion US dollars.[11] The infrastructure that had taken the Japanese over a decade to build was demolished within weeks. It was said that the Japanese came to build and the Russians came to destroy.

At this time, not only were the Japanese subject to violence from the Russians but also from Chinese mobs intent on revenge against their former oppressors. The Japanese had succeeded in controlling the insurgency groups in Manchuria because of their superior forces and their honest and efficient government. To the ordinary Manchurian farmer, feelings of patriotism became subdued and they returned to "docile obedience" as the Japanese-run system proved to be superior to the corruption and disorder of the former Chinese regime.[12] Japanese houses were gutted for firewood and their inhabitants beaten and killed. Former policemen were particularly targeted.[13] The Japanese, who had lived segregated from the Manchurians, began desperately fleeing their homes.

Fearful for his family's safety, Dr Takayama made arrangements for their evacuation to the countryside in late August. It was a testament to the doctor's standing with the natives that a Manchurian friend was willing to risk his own safety in order to help them. Leaving Yu-san to guard the clinic, the family relocated to a house in Dingbu (頂埔) where they managed to escape the violence and disorder of the cities.

A few weeks later, believing the worst was over, the family returned to Tetsurei, but the situation remained precarious. Though better off than the true Japanese, as Taiwanese living in the Japanese part of town the Takayamas were vulnerable. Throughout Manchuria, many Taiwanese had stopped speaking Japanese in public. Few residents ventured out except to sell goods and buy essentials during daytime.

As summer shifted into autumn and then winter, the Takayamas spent their days locked inside the house with only occasional contact with their friends. Though Dr Takayama had substantial savings in the bank, the Japanese yen had become worthless once Japanese assets were frozen. Russian military notes and the Chinese yuan came into effect. The doctor bitterly regretted not having converted his money into gold and silver earlier. Somehow, with the help of friends, he managed to keep the family from starvation as he searched for a way out of Manchuria.

When the loud knocking sounded at noon, Dr Takayama assumed it was one of his acquaintances. He would not have dared open the door at night. Akihisa and his younger brother, Tadahisa, trailed behind their father as he went to the door. A blast of icy air hit them and they found themselves staring into the barrel of a pistol. It was the first time Akihisa had ever seen a gun up close. The gaping black hole of the metallic instrument held him spellbound. His eyes widened and he found himself unable to breathe. Dr Takayama took a surprised step back into the foyer and nearly knocked Akihisa over.

The two uniformed Russian soldiers pushed their way in and closed the door. To Akihisa, they looked gigantic. Both clean-shaven, one wore the khaki uniform of the lower ranks. The other looked like an officer. He had on a fur hat and wore a clean greatcoat with shiny brass buttons on top of his "Tsarist green" uniform. It was he who pointed the gun at Dr Takayama.

"часы!"[14] The officer tapped his left wrist three times with the tip of his handgun then swiftly pointed the pistol back at the family.

Dr Takayama did not move. Akihisa noticed his father's right hand was shaking. He had never seen his father so frightened before. This was the same man whom Akihisa had once seen suturing his own big toe without anaesthetic after accidentally stepping on a broken bottle. The same man who had so ably kept their family from harm all through the war. His father's fear heightened Akihisa's terror. He grasped his younger brother's hand and edged back toward the wall. The movement seemed to irritate the officer and he aimed the gun at the children. The soldier pushed his way past the Takayamas toward the bedrooms. Dr Takayama looked after him worriedly but there was little he could do.

"часы!" the officer yelled. He cocked the pistol.

Akihisa's hands felt damp. His father quickly removed the watch from his wrist and handed it to the man. The officer examined the watch and slipped it into his coat pocket.

Of course, Akihisa thought. He had heard so many stories of how the Russian soldiers loved watches. Some had collections that covered the lengths of their arms. Now that they've gotten what they came for, maybe they'll leave. Akihisa let out his breath and relaxed his hold on Tadahisa.

But the two men were not finished. They stomped in their high boots throughout the house, looking under tatami mats and empty-ing drawers, searching for valuables. There was little to take by this point. Much of what the family owned had gone toward financing the necessities of life: food and fuel. The wartime rations of salt, sugar, and rice counted as luxuries now. Kaoliang was the staple grain and they were lucky to have that and the coal. There were people who burned asphalt from the streets in order to stay warm.

Dr Takayama followed the men at a distance as they made their way through the house. For the first time, Akihisa wondered how his father had managed to keep their family alive and how they would survive without the head of the household. Though he was often cowed by his father's hair-trigger irritability and verbal blasts, Akihisa knew he would be devastated if he lost his father. The Russians were known to kill for no reason at all. He wanted his father to come back to the foyer and not follow the men around. He sank down on his haunches and huddled on the wooden floor, crossing his arms around his legs.

Due to a trick of his memory, Akihisa would not be able to remember later whether his mother and sister were with them that day. It was a subject not often spoken about. "We were scared stiff" was the usual extent of the conversations on the rare occasion that the topic arose. It was only after consulting his siblings during the writing of this biography that he found out from his younger brother that the whole family had indeed been together during the home invasion. While the officer was in the foyer, his subordinate had corralled Mrs Takayama and the two youngest children into a bedroom. Trying to shield her son and daughter, Mrs Takayama had backed the group into a corner of the room with her arms outspread. That action earned her a rap on her hand from the soldier's pistol. Thinking back on the events of that night, Akihisa realized how fortunate the women of his family had been on that occasion. Rapes by Soviet soldiers were rampant.

There was one brutal account that was spoken of that Akihisa later found particularly disturbing. It involved the arrival of a refugee family of five at the Shinkyō[15] train station. The Japanese woman carried a baby on her back and was accompanied by three young daughters. The woman and oldest girl carried their few belongings—some cloth bags and a straw mat. As they crossed the square to enter the station, the family was surrounded by a group of seven or eight Russian soldiers. The men set upon the family and took turns raping the woman and girls while the abandoned baby wailed. After they were done, the soldiers lined the family up in a row on the ground and shot them dead. None of the terrified spectators dared to intervene for fear of their own lives.[16]

From the start of the invasion in August up to their departure in April of the following year, Soviet soldiers had raped countless women, not discriminating between Japanese and Manchurian. There were even reports of female Soviet soldiers raping conquered men.[17] One Taiwanese doctor recalled feeling despair after refusing an abortion to a Chinese rape victim who was six months pregnant.[18] In mainly futile efforts to escape detection, women and girls began to cut their hair, blacken their faces, and dress like boys. Most women stayed indoors as much as practicable but even that was not a guarantee of safety. A late night knock was a sure sign of Soviet soldiers seeking women and valuables.

After what seemed like an eternity, Dr Takayama returned to the foyer and looked down at his cowering children.

"They're gone," he said matter-of-factly, the strain of the encounter still visible on his gaunt face.

Apparently, the Russians had made their way into the adjoining medical clinic, and seeing the equipment, realized that Dr Takayama was doing "humanitarian" work and so had quietly departed through the clinic doors. The Takayamas had gotten off lightly.

This encounter would reinforce Akihisa's bias against Russians.

But even more than his personal experiences, the moral code that Akihisa Takayama had imbibed from his Japanese education during his formative years prohibited him from warming to the Soviets. For him, it was unconscionable for the Russians to take Japanese soldiers to Siberia for forced labour, in defiance of the Geneva Convention. That his brother's favourite teacher, Mr Seno, had been one of those soldiers and suffered for years in Siberia strengthened his sense of injustice. To his Japanese self, agreements were to be honoured, but government actions, Russian and otherwise, frequently frustrated his beliefs. To him, Russians would remain the thugs of his adolescence and though he would later befriend the odd Russian, he would not be able to forsake his initial impressions.

· 4 ·

Yu-san's Disappearance

They came in the middle of the night, banging at the entrance.

"Lin Yu-san! Open the door!"

The Takayamas stirred on their tatami mats and hastily wrapped their quilts around themselves. Now that spring had arrived, they had stopped wearing coats in the house but they did not warm the house at night in order to save coal and the chill of the night air hit them hard. They still had to wear sweaters over their pyjamas and thick socks to go to bed.

The banging continued, louder this time. Dr Takayama hurried to the door as he struggled to put on his coat.

Akihisa was slow to wake. His younger brother, Tadahisa, wrapped in a quilt beside him, was even slower. Their younger sister and brother were in a room further down the hall next to their parents' room. They could hear sounds coming from Yu-san's room next door. Akihisa and Tadahisa ran over to his room and slid open the *shōji*. Yu-san was not there. Even his bedding was gone.

The shouting drew closer, as did the sound of boots approaching. The two boys ran back to their room and scrambled to the furthest tatami mat from the doorway. They pulled up their quilts and waited.

Were these men Communists or Nationalists?

Akihisa's father had not taught him much about the current political situation. His paltry knowledge was gleaned from eavesdropping on his father's few conversations with visitors who came to the house. Because his parents and Yu-san spoke Taiwanese among themselves, Akihisa could not clearly understand what they said. The Japanese newspapers and radio that Akihisa could understand were no longer available. Even if they were, Akihisa doubted he would be able to make sense of what was going on. It seemed as if Communist and Nationalist soldiers came and went out of Tetsurei arbitrarily. Nobody knew who was in charge at any time, now that the Soviets were gone. It was only as an adult that Akihisa was able to piece together a picture of what had been going on.

In 1911, republican forces had risen up against the Qing government to end a millenniums-old dynasty. The political leader of the new Republic of China, Sun Yat-Sen, favoured a Western-style parliamentary democracy. Because he lacked the military strength, he resigned his presidency to General Yuan Shih-kai, the former Imperial War Minister and commander of the most powerful army in the country. Elections were held and the newly formed Kuomintang (KMT or Nationalist) party won a majority in both houses. However, Yuan turned out to be a dictator, to the point of assassinating opponents and declaring himself emperor.[1] Province after province protested his rule by declaring independence. Upon Yuan's death in 1916,[2] provincial governors across China struggled for control. Thus began the Warlord Era and a period of near anarchy.[3]

Sun Yat-Sen felt that a Kuomintang army was needed to bring China under the control of a central government. He turned to Communist Russia for help, but assistance was forthcoming only on condition that he cooperate with the Chinese Communists. Formed from humble beginnings in 1921, the Chinese Communist Party (CCP) led by Mao Zedong had gained enough followers to challenge the ruling Kuomintang.[4] The two parties reluctantly amalgamated in 1923 to create the National Revolutionary Army under the command of Chiang Kai-Shek in order to drive out foreign powers and to unite China. Sun's early death in 1925 endangered the fragile alliance between the Communists and KMT but the united front persisted.[5]

After successfully defeating the warlords of China's north and northeast[6] in the Northern Expedition of 1926-27, Chiang turned against the Communists and conducted a brutal purge beginning with the Shanghai Massacre of 1927.[7] An estimated 300,000 Communists and dissidents were killed over the next year.[8] The Communists resisted by turning to guerrilla warfare and instigating peasant rebellions. The Chinese civil war would continue through the next decade.[9] The Nationalists came close to defeating the Communists at times but the CCP persisted. One frequently cited example of Communist survival is the Long March of 1934, in which Mao led his soldiers in a year-long trek over difficult terrain to establish a new base in the north-western province of Shaanxi after his eastern bases were wiped out by the KMT.

The Marco Polo Bridge Incident[10] of 1937 sparked the Second Sino-Japanese War, and the Nationalists and Communists agreed to form a united front against the Japanese despite their deep mutual animosity. After the war, attempts by the Americans to broker a political solution and a possible coalition government were unsuccessful. The Nationalists were the official government of China, but the Communists refused to recognize their authority.

In August 1945, after the Japanese surrender, the Communists and Nationalists began to jockey for dominance, particularly in Manchuria and northern China. Chiang was unwilling to let the

Soviets or the Chinese Communists accept the surrender from Japanese officers, and he sought help from the United States to airlift Nationalist soldiers into the recovered regions. Washington's assistance clearly marked its support for Chiang and the Nationalists. This led to a resurgence of the civil war that had been covert during the campaign against the Japanese.[11] The Soviets occupied Manchuria in the interim.

By September, Communist forces had moved into Manchuria and were organizing themselves. Despite American aid, Chiang was unable to move enough Nationalist forces into Manchuria, therefore he requested a delay in the withdrawal of Soviet forces.[12] The Russians complied and installed Chiang's appointees in the major cities.

But the Russians were playing a duplicitous political game. While purporting to honour the treaties of "Friendship and Alliance," which deemed the Nationalists the legitimate government in Manchuria,[13] Stalin sought to help his Chinese Communist comrades to seize power. To this end, Soviet troops helped Mao's units take the Shanhaiguan mountain pass on the Manchurian border and cities along the railway line in Manchuria. They quietly allowed the Chinese Communists access to weapons and supplies left by the Japanese and helped them set up local administrative centres. The Soviets reportedly equipped several hundred thousand Communists at this time while trying not to compromise their diplomatic standing with the Nationalists and their American allies.[14]

In December 1945, American president Harry Truman sent General George Marshall[15] to try and broker a deal between the two factions. The parties arrived at a tentative ceasefire and military unification agreement in February 1946. But by the time that Yu-san Lin was being sought by the soldiers, the Nationalists and Communists, disregarding the ceasefire, had already turned parts of Manchuria into battlegrounds. Full-scale civil war would begin between

Kuomintang forces and the newly named People's Liberation Army in June 1946.[16]

For Akihisa, the transitions were bewildering and terrifying. When the soldiers came into his room, Akihisa saw that they were Nationalists. They wore dark overcoats and the tan uniforms of infantrymen. On their heads were steel helmets with the Republic of China symbol: a white sun in a blue sky. The three proceeded to open cupboards and flip back tatami mats to expose the wooden boards below. All the while, they kept shouting, "Lin Yu-san!"

Now that the Nationalists were "in charge" of Manchuria, they felt free to recruit men for their troops as they had done in the rest of China. The Japanese had kept meticulous census records and it was presumably from those that new soldiers were being recruited. As a young man of Chinese ethnicity, Yu-san would have been seen as a viable recruit.

Support for the Nationalists had declined in the cities because of corruption. The brutality of Chiang's secret police did little to boost support for the KMT.[17] Stories of forced recruitment were common.[18] Men were kidnapped as they went about their daily activities, and were sometimes heard from by their families years later, if at all.[19] The fear of forced service was real.

But where had Yu-san gone? He had retired to his room as usual last night but had now disappeared. Akihisa could hear the soldiers searching the rest of the house and expected to hear a triumphant shout at any moment. But the only sounds were those of the soldiers sliding open *shōji* and slamming close cupboard doors.

"Lin Yu-san. Come out right now!" a soldier shouted, so close to Akihisa that he jumped. The man had returned for a second look at the room. Akihisa wasn't sure if he understood what the man had said in Mandarin. He knew his cousin's name but the second sentence was a mere guess since he had only started at the Chinese school recently. Having decided to try and return to Taiwan as soon as possible, Dr Takayama had enrolled the two older boys in Chinese school in anticipation of their education in Taiwan. The two younger children he kept at home since his daughter was only in Grade Two and his youngest son had just started Kindergarten. Like many Japanese in Manchuria, he had been trying to get his family out of China since the Japanese surrender.

After months of being cooped up at home, Akihisa welcomed the prospect of leaving the house. The first day of school had seen the two boys put on Western clothing, winter coats, and their square leather backpacks from the Japanese school to walk into the Manchurian part of town. They wrinkled their noses at the dirt and smells in the Chinese quarter as they made their way to school.

Akihisa knew they had made a mistake when they entered the old brick building. All the other students wore the quilted jackets and pants of the Chinese. The Takayamas were the only non-Manchurians and their backpacks and Western clothes loudly advertised that fact. The two were directed to their respective classrooms; Tadahisa was two grades below his fourteen-year-old brother. Sitting at his desk surrounded by over forty students in a room heated only by a coal stove, Akihisa missed the centrally heated Japanese schools that he had attended in Hōten and Tetsurei. The Chinese boys eating steamed buns and dumplings also noticed his sushi bento, though they left him alone during the lunch hour.

There was a platform fronting the blackboard where the teacher delivered his lessons, but Akihisa didn't know what the Chinese teacher was saying most of the time. The only thing that he was sure of was his Chinese name (Cheng-Chao), but he wasn't even able to get that right. Because the teacher's Mandarin accent sounded different from his father's, Akihisa had missed answering the first time when the teacher called his name during morning attendance. The day was interminable and incomprehensible. Lunch was eaten inside the classrooms so Akihisa was not able to see how his brother had fared. Later Tadahisa told him of an incident that had occurred.

At lunch, a group of boys had gathered around Tadahisa's desk to examine the novelty in their midst. One of them was taller than the rest.

"*Hanjian!*"[20] the Manchurian boy spat, his face screwed up in disgust.

The other boys standing with him sneered. Bundled in their padded Chinese jackets, the boys looked like quilted blue sausages.

Tadahisa didn't know what the word meant.

Seeing his confusion, one of the other boys wrote the Chinese characters out on a piece of paper but Tadahisa was still baffled.

"*Hanjian, gai si le!*" The boy raised his right arm and mimed shooting Tadahisa in the head with a pistol. The others pretended to fire on Tadahisa with rifles.

Tadahisa remained silent. The boys formed a tighter circle around his desk. He clenched his fists and prepared for a fight.

Fortunately, the class monitor had appeared at that moment and pushed the boys away.

Akihisa understood that the term *hanjian* meant "traitor to China." The epithet had been hurled at the two Takayama boys over the last few days. Previously, Akihisa had only encountered outright racism when he was once called チヤンコロ (清國奴) or "Qing slave" by an older boy at school. Though he had been shocked at the unexpected hostility that implied, nothing worse had happened. But now, as he emerged from the cocoon of Japanese privilege and protection, the antagonism of the Manchurian Chinese was as startling for Akihisa as the bigotry he'd encountered from the Japanese.

Now, as Akihisa tried to decipher what the Nationalist soldiers were saying, he wondered if his family would be labelled *hanjian* if Yu-san failed to appear. The concept was difficult for him to grasp. The obvious example of Wang Jingwei was easy enough to understand. The former Nationalist politician had been a staunch patriot who worked closely with Sun Yat-Sen. After Sun's death, Wang unsuccessfully vied with Chiang Kai-Shek for dominance in the Kuomintang, eventually losing control to Chiang and the conservative elements of the party. Advocating for a peaceful solution to the Second Sino-Japanese War, Wang established a collaborationist government with the Japanese. He was widely regarded as a traitor by both the Nationalists and Communists.

But how did the label apply to ordinary people like the Takayamas? After fifty years of being Japanese citizens, the Taiwanese had suddenly found themselves under Chinese rule. Did changing their Chinese names to Japanese ones mean that they had betrayed their Chinese heritage? Akihisa knew he was now supposedly Chinese but he felt no affinity with the Chinese students at school. His feeling of alienation surfaced each time he struggled to speak Mandarin.

Did neighbours helping neighbours qualify as treason? There were Chinese Manchurians who helped Japanese police officers survive mob attacks.[21] A Taiwanese family had hidden Japanese spies in their home until they could be repatriated. Akihisa's own father had written a fake medical excuse for a young woman so she could escape service in the Nationalist army. He had also been the guarantor for a Japanese couple falsely accused by the Chinese of keeping firearms in their home. Which deeds were treason and which were acts of humanity?

Dr Takayama did not fear being singled out for profiteering or being charged as a political *hanjian* since he had no connections with the Nationalists and the bulk of his savings had been lost. He was merely one of the many victims of the war who was trying to do the best he could for his family. On this particular night, all he wished to do was protect Yu-san from being absorbed into the Nationalist military. He and his wife gathered the two youngest children in their room and waited for the three men to complete their search. When the men finally departed with a loud bang of the front door, the

Takayamas heaved a collective sigh of relief.

Still baffled by Yu-san's disappearance, Akihisa and Tadahisa crept next door. Dr Takayama was already in the room calling out Yu-san's name, telling him it was safe, and straightening the tatami mats. The two boys climbed up on the mats and circled the room still as confused as before. Then they heard a scrabbling sound coming from the *oshiire* where the bedding was usually stored. Akihisa ran across the expanse of the three mats and watched opened-mouthed as Yu-san climbed out of the storage cupboard using the shelving as a stepladder. Somehow, as soon as the soldiers arrived, he'd had the presence of mind to shove his bedding into the closet, scale the shelves, and wedge himself in the small space under the rafters.

Having successfully dodged service in the Japanese army prior to coming to Manchuria, Yu-san had now narrowly escaped being press-ganged by the Chinese military. He hoped his luck would hold. When daylight broke, he would make his way to Mukden to find shelter with the Taiwanese Association there, hoping the larger city would afford him anonymity while he and the Takayamas tried to find a way out of Manchuria.

Leaving Manchuria

TAIWAN STRAIT, SEPTEMBER 1946

Akihisa tried to find a comfortable position in the cramped cargo hold of the 500-ton wooden freighter. Tadahisa had already fallen asleep next to him, and his parents, cradling the two youngest children in their laps, also seemed to be resting. Yu-san, with his head on a suitcase, had his eyes closed though Akihisa wasn't certain of what he had seen in the brief flash of light that had illuminated the hold when someone escaped to spend the night on deck. Akihisa wished he too could leave this dark hole stinking of vomit and unwashed bodies but his father had given strict orders for them to remain together. Besides, he didn't relish the thought of picking his way through the vomitus of his fellow seasick travellers. Rough seas had taken its toll on most of the passengers but mops and buckets were in short supply. Accustomed to Japanese hygiene standards, the dirt and grime since their departure from home had been distasteful for his entire family and particularly trying for his mother, who still tried to keep the children as clean as possible under the circumstances.

Thanks to the United Nations Relief and Rehabilitation Administration, the Takayamas had been able to reunite with Yu-san at the Mukden Taiwanese Association building in June. It was a bright day when Akihisa and his family, each of them carrying a single suitcase or bundle, left for the Tieling train station. His father's suitcase contained documents, money, and other valuables while his mother's held her jewellery and some photographs—years of hard work condensed into a couple of cases. Akihisa's suitcase held some of the clothes that would see them through the trip. He had been glad when they met up with Yu-san, and his cousin had taken up the bulk of the family load of bedding and cookware, but his arms were still tired from dragging the case on and off trains and boats.

Perhaps because of his fluency in Chinese, the Relief Administration had put Dr Takayama in charge of a group of more than thirty people for the journey south. Akihisa was later to find out that there were at least ten such Taiwanese groups leaving Manchuria, ranging in size from small cohorts such as the Takayamas' to groups as large as two hundred. Typically, men were tasked with guarding the luggage from thieves while the women took care of the children.

Akihisa tried again to stretch out but there was little room through the tangled legs of his brother. He shifted his head on the suitcase he was using as a pillow and tried to sleep but to no avail. His mind kept turning to the home he had just left. He had spent twelve of his fourteen years in Manchuria and did not know what awaited him in Taiwan. As they walked to the Tieling train station, Akihisa had taken one last look at the home he would never see again. The house with clinic that the Takayamas occupied was set inside a fenced compound which included not only their building but also a smaller house in which the Japanese pharmacist, Mr Goto, and his wife lived. Also in the compound was an abandoned chapel that might have served one of the Christian missions active in Manchuria since the late 1800s. Akihisa thought it might also have been a Korean church at one time. Though some missionaries attempted to remain in China while the Nationalists were in charge, by the time the Communists came to power in 1949, there was no room for them. During the years that the Takayamas occupied the compound, Akihisa had never seen any activity in the chapel.

At the time of the Takayamas' departure from Manchuria, the Nationalists were losing the war both politically and militarily. In Manchuria, as in the rest of China, Nationalist officers who had arrived in the postwar takeover of Japanese properties proved to be greedy and corrupt. Eyewitness accounts in Mukden painted a picture of grasping, avaricious KMT behaviour. Most public buildings meant for government use fell into private ownership under Nationalist officials. The situation was exacerbated by the undisciplined Nationalist soldiers, who had taken to robbing civilians. The Manchurian Chinese began to see the Central Government men as no better than their previous occupiers, the rapacious Russians. The Nationalists were losing not only the Northeast but the goodwill of the Chinese people.[1]

Even worse for the government's reputation was the decision to retain former collaborators in positions of power despite the anti-*hanjian* policy. The Chinese who had just fought a fiercely nationalistic war against the Japanese and who reviled *hanjian* were aghast to see Li Shuo-hsin, former Minister of War in the puppet Mongolian government, appointed commander of the Nationalist Tenth Route Army; Chao Pao-yuan, former Manchukuo Army commander, become head of the Anti-Communist Army in Chiaotung; and Japanese collaborator, Chiang Peng-fei, take over the Twenty-Seventh Army.[2] And the Nationalists were slow in punishing Japanese war criminals.[3]

Meanwhile, the Communists were making great gains in converting ordinary people to their cause. Their soldiers were well-schooled in Communist doctrine and their forces avoided antagonizing the populace through robbery since they were paid directly with food instead of money, thus partially avoiding the problems of inflation. When the Takayamas left Mukden in mid-1946, the city was still a KMT stronghold and Nationalist troops outnumbered the Communists three to one. By the end of the year, the three million strong KMT military had decreased to 2.6 million. Many of the Nationalist soldiers had defected to the Communists.[4]

After the Takayamas arrived in Mukden, they had stayed for a short time with the local Taiwanese Association before being transported to Tianjin in northern China. Their passenger train displayed banners declaring that the passengers within were Taiwanese, presumably to distinguish them from the Japanese who were finally being repatriated. Many of the Japanese who had survived the Soviet occupation and harsh Manchurian winter in the big cities were conveyed in open railcars to the closest port and frequently endured stoning by Chinese along the tracks who hurled abuse at their former "oppressors."

Despite the hardships that the Takayamas had gone through, Akihisa thought they were fortunate in comparison to most Japanese. As in any war, it was the common people who suffered most. The fate of the Japanese in Manchuria helped to cultivate Akihisa's lifelong belief in the futility of war. The settlers who had left Japan with hopes of bettering their lives and of helping their country expand found themselves bewildered victims of brutal victors. The lands that the Japanese had acquired were returned to the Chinese soaked with the blood of Japanese colonists. Aside from deaths at the hands of Soviet soldiers and Chinese civilians as well as the mass suicides when news of the Japanese defeat arrived, the survivors paid a heavy price. Those who managed to make it to the big cities in Manchuria often succumbed to disease, starvation, and cold in poorly equipped refugee camps. One Taiwanese described the transformation of a Japanese elementary school that sheltered thinly clothed refugees into a tomb as the winter wore on.[5] A park in Mukden,[6] where locals used to boat in the summer and skate in the winter, became a burial ground for Japanese victims.[7] In many cases, the Japanese refugees who managed to reach their ancestral lands found relatives unable to care for them when they arrived. The repatriates were only allowed to bring back what they could carry and one thousand yen per person.[8] Agricultural settlers who had migrated to Manchukuo in the 1930s frequently returned to family farms in worse condition than before their departure.

Most of the Japanese who remained in Manchuria had to depend on help from the Chinese. Local peasants adopted some of the war orphans and desperate Japanese women married Chinese nationals or worked as servants for Chinese families. The number of abandoned women and children may have been as high as 20,000. Because of China's isolation and the Cold War, these war orphans and wives were not allowed to visit Japan until 1972. Though some chose to be repatriated at that time, their long stays in China made for a difficult adjustment. The number of repatriates and immigrants had reached 100,000 by the mid-2000s, though many struggled to fit into the lifestyles of modern Japan.[9]

When Akihisa later learned of the fate of the Manchurian Japanese, he was thankful for his Taiwanese status despite his earlier yearning to be truly Japanese. Their ethnic origins had also saved his father from participating in the Sino-Japanese War. One day, while the war was still in full force, Akihisa had overheard his father complaining to a Taiwanese physician friend about their pseudo-Japanese status. Dr Takayama had felt slighted by the Japanese because he was not chosen to work at his alma mater; he had aspired to be a research professor at the university. It later turned out that Manchu Medical University was the site of war crimes from which Dr Takayama had been fortunate to be excluded.

The medical college's original function had been to introduce superior Japanese medical practices to the locals and immigrant Japanese farmers and thus prevent the spread of malaria, cholera, and the plague in Manchuria. Travelling medical students dispensed health advice at various training centres along the South Manchurian Railway. The university also focused on research into the endemic diseases of Manchuria and Mongolia, including typhus, tuberculosis, and haemorrhagic fever.[10] However, during the war, some experiments were conducted on healthy Chinese nationals. Reportedly, "extremely cruel vivisections" were performed and fresh and healthy brain samples taken from adults without any history of mental illness for psychology experiments.[11]

The medical college was part of the Ishii Network, headed by Shirō Ishii, a surgeon and senior medical officer in the Kwantung Army. Ignoring the 1925 Geneva Protocol banning the use of chemical and biological weapons, Ishii decided to exploit the potential of biological weapons and applied to the military for permission to conduct clandestine research. As a result he created a network of military medical research institutions based in Manchuria, including the infamous Unit 731.

At least three thousand experimental victims, most of them Chinese, including women and children, were rounded up by the Japanese army and transferred to the unit. Some of these human guinea pigs, known as *maruta* or "logs," were subjected to infection with haemorrhagic fever, anthrax, the plague, typhus, dysentery, and cholera.

In August 1945, when it was evident that defeat was imminent, Ishii ordered Unit 731 blown up, the "logs" killed, and all documents burned. The staff and their families were transported via the South Manchurian Railway to Dairen and subsequently repatriated to Japan.[12] Most of the military doctors and scientists of the Ishii Network were not charged with war crimes. In fact, many of them went on to hold important positions in the Japanese medical establishment after the war.[13]

For the Taiwanese in 1945, now under a Chinese government, it was easy to say that they were not responsible for the actions of their colonizers. Still, for teenagers like Akihisa, whose early identities had been forged in the fires of Japanese ultra-nationalism, the effects lingered. It was difficult to reconcile the orderly, civilized society that he had experienced under Japanese rule with the atrocities committed by the Japanese in the war. Condemning Japanese actions was like condemning a part of themselves. Japanese was Akihisa's first language and Japan would remain a part of his identity no matter how his self-concept evolved in later life. Pride in Japanese culture and achievements as well as a propensity to speak Japanese would form an enduring part of his personality. He would continue to speak mainly Japanese with Tadahisa for the rest of his life.

"Tadahisa, move over," Akihisa whispered to his sleeping brother. Tadahisa stirred but made no extra space. Akihisa shoved him away but his brother immediately moved back to his prior position. Finally, Akihisa gave up and scrunched himself up into a ball then thumped his head back onto the suitcase. He would have to make do in the dank heat of this stinking hole. They'd been treated like cargo since they left home and tonight wasn't any different. Morning couldn't come soon enough.

But at least they were free to speak Japanese on board the ship without fear of being mistaken for Japanese aliens. Throughout their journey, Dr Takayama had admonished the group whenever they were in public and a Japanese phrase slipped out. Though Mandarin would have been preferable, most of the families could only speak Taiwanese and that was the language to which they resorted. Akihisa was silent for most of the trip, except when they were confined to their living quarters. When they arrived in Tianjin, the local Taiwanese Association president[14] had directed them to a nearby temple. They'd laid down their bedding on concrete floors and set up their cookware to wait out the week before they could board a boat south to Shanghai.

In Shanghai, the head of the Taiwanese Association had taken them to an empty factory where they stayed for several weeks before they boarded this boat.[15] Akihisa had only been able to catch glimpses of the teeming, modern city before they were hustled into the warehouse. Shiny chauffeur-driven Rolls-Royces threaded their way through thoroughfares populated by beggars and barefoot men pulling rickshaws and pedicabs. Noodle vendors shared sidewalk space with the front doors of expensive restaurants. The sight of so many French, British, Russian, American, and exotic-looking European faces left Akihisa open-mouthed despite having previously encountered Western features in the Russians he had seen in Manchuria. But in both Tianjin and Shanghai, Akihisa had not been able to see the cities properly, for the group had been advised that it would be safer not to venture out.

The Chinese civil war was being fought in the interior provinces in the summer of 1946, and the citizens of Shanghai went about their daily activities seemingly unperturbed. But the Takayamas felt vulnerable. This was a common feeling among Taiwanese repatriates.[16] They were not used to the sharp and unscrupulous business practices of the Chinese cities. Wariness in doing business was a lesson they had to learn as they came into increasing contact with their Chinese compatriots.

Akihisa's stomach growled. It seemed that he'd been hungry for a long time, ever since they had left home. He wished he had more of the *mantous* that they'd been given in Shanghai. His younger sister couldn't stop remarking how delicious the Chinese breads were. The *mantous* had been a welcome change from the *muei* (Chinese porridge) on which they had been subsisting for so long. Watery rice gruel without much else was the staple for most Taiwanese refugees. By the time Akihisa looked back to this time in his life, his parents were dead and he couldn't ask them how they had coped in matters of food. It was more than likely that they had gone without and saved the best for their children.

Finally they were on the last leg of their two-month-long journey. Akihisa would remember none of China's landmarks, save one. The sight of the Great Wall on one side and the ocean on the other as their train passed through Shanhaiguan into China was to remain with him for life. They had weathered long train rides, interminable waits, concrete mattresses, a typhoon, hunger, and constant uncertainty. Barring an accident, they were expected to reach the Taiwanese port of Keelung in the morning. He couldn't wait to be on dry, solid land. His life as Akihisa was over and he would now have to re-invent himself as Cheng-Chao Yang. The tide of history was sweeping him from the only life that he had ever known to the "homeland" that he did not remember and was completely unprepared for.

Part II

Taiwan
1946-1959
Cheng-Chao Yang

Culture Shock

Cheng-Chao, formerly Akihisa Takayama, scurried along the dirt path that was crowded with undergrowth. He would have to hurry if he were to catch the early train to school. He still needed to eat his breakfast and change into his school uniform. As usual he'd prepared his school satchel the night before, but his mother had yet to slip his aluminum lunch box inside. She was annoyed that he'd allowed the water urn to get so low, barely enough for her to fill the pot for congee this morning. Uncharacteristically, he had forgotten to fetch water the night before. She'd dispatched him on his chore as soon as he hopped off his bed at six. Though there was a well near their house, the water was not potable because of its high salinity. Cheng-Chao had to make the quarter-mile trek from their house to the well every few days to carry back wooden buckets of fresh water. The landowner, on whose courtyard it sat, allowed several families in Yongkang Village to draw water from it. The ancestral Yang family home had been part of this southern Taiwanese rural town in Tainan

County for several generations.

Cheng-Chao was shocked by the primitiveness of the Yang house when they arrived. Built by Cheng-Chao's great-grandfather, the Chinese-style house was already past its prime when Dr Yang's family left for Manchuria, and it had become more decrepit in the years since 1934. Although the grounds were close to 6000 square feet, the actual living space was about 1400 square feet, of which only half was available to the Yangs, the rest being closed off for storage. Cheng-Chao's parents occupied one of the small bedrooms and the four children shared the other. A small kitchen and ancestral hall completed the living quarters. Given difficult postwar conditions in Taiwan, the family had been fortunate to be allocated the residence upon their return.

Cheng-Chao filled the buckets and hurried back as quickly as he could. His mother was already in the front yard with a basin and washboard scrubbing the family laundry. His father and siblings were seated on wooden stools around a small table having congee in front of the ancestral hall. The "hall" barely held an altar for ancestor worship and two carved chairs. Cheng-Chao was still not accustomed to the humid, tropical weather, which allowed them to eat outdoors even in the winter. Had they been in Manchuria, they would have donned their woollen underwear long ago. He would always remember his first sight of Taiwan, the blue skies, blue-green waters, and lush green hills as they landed in Keelung Harbour. Their train ride south to Tainan had been a blur of paddy fields, craggy rocks, and verdant mountainsides as they sped past family farms and small towns. Some of the Japanese-built railways and factories were still operating, though not as efficiently as under the Japanese.

By the time they made it to their ancestral home via ox and cart, Cheng-Chao was so overwhelmed by the new sights and exhausted by their long journey that he'd not registered the worn tiles, crumbling brickwork, and shabby furniture which gave the abode its overall dinginess. All he'd noticed was the lack of space and complete loss of privacy. But in the past two months, Cheng-Chao had gotten used to using the outhouse, taking sponge baths with water heated on the wood-burning kitchen stove, sleeping on a platform bed that creaked as the four children tossed in the cramped space under mosquito netting, and doing his homework seated on a bamboo stool by the light of a single naked lightbulb. How he missed the running water, flush toilets, and spacious rooms of his Manchurian home! Though telephones, gas stoves, modern plumbing, and other conveniences were available on the island, the Yang residence had been neglected and allowed to lag behind like many Qing dynasty buildings in the poor, rural areas of Taiwan.

Cheng-Chao emptied the bucket into the water barrel that stood by the threshold of the soot-blackened kitchen which fitted only a small brick stove and a tiny table pushed against the wall. He ladled out some water into a plastic basin, then washed his face and brushed his teeth before going out to the breakfast table. The younger children had already finished their congee and were getting ready for school. His father sat alone, nursing a cup of tea. Dr Yang looked haggard, as did his wife. Wrinkles had begun to appear on their thirty-eight-year-old faces. Traces of the well-dressed social dancer that was Dr Yang and the pretty young woman at the forefront of Western-style fashions still remained, but their youth was rapidly being swallowed by the cares of survival.

Besides protecting Japan's southern reaches from attack by its neighbours, Taiwan had been an economic boon for the Japanese. As Japan's first colony, Taiwan fulfilled the typical role of colonies worldwide by exporting raw materials to the imperialist power and serving as a ready market for Japanese goods. Rich in natural resources, the Taiwanese had already been developing their economy before the

1895 takeover, but Japanese know-how and investment sped up the process. Determined to make Taiwan into a showcase colony and flush from the reparations of the Russo-Japanese War, the Japanese government invested heavily in capital infrastructure projects such as railways and dams. Taiwan began producing sugar and rice in vast quantities for Japanese consumption. Government assistance to sugar farms and mills as well as the construction of railways allowed this already important industry to grow rapidly. Other sectors which also benefitted from efficient Japanese administration and financial investment included camphor, sulphur, coal, gold, salt, tea, indigo, pineapples, bananas, plantains, and hemp.[2] These successes generated significant tax revenues for the Japanese government.

After its unconditional surrender, Japan lost a prosperous colony, and Taiwan lost the standard of living, one of the highest in Asia, that it had enjoyed. Taiwan now faced the immediate problem of trying to rebuild its infrastructure. American bombing raids had destroyed significant portions of the buildings that were constructed during Japanese rule. By the end of World War II, more than half of the railways and roadways were unusable. Over two hundred factories had been bombed and vital industries were crippled. Three of the island's four electric power plants had been razed.[3] The civilians, who had survived the war on government-controlled rations, now found it difficult to make ends meet under China, because of its economic problems. Hyperinflation resulting from the civil war on the mainland made government-issued tender increasingly useless. The gains made under Japanese administration rapidly disappeared.[4]

Nationalist troops and government officials who arrived in 1945 to accept the Japanese handover did not see the local Taiwanese as compatriots who had been liberated, but as "Japanese slaves," whose thinking had been tainted by half a century of Japanese rule. Taiwanese people and property were their spoils of war.[5] But when the first troops arrived in October 1945, they were warmly welcomed by the Taiwanese; the crowds holding up the welcome banners were met by raw recruits with worn clothing, carrying pots, pans, and bedding on bamboo rods. These poorly paid, uncouth recruits in no time took over schools, temples, and hospitals and proceeded to live off the locals. They had not seen modern conveniences such as telephones, electricity, cars, and running water. Looting and harassment of the locals, especially the Japanese who had not yet been repatriated, became common.[6] Senior KMT officers began to enrich themselves with Japanese properties. Even though the Japanese had been brutal in their governance, they had not been avaricious, as these newcomers were.[7,8]

Whenever Cheng-Chao thought back to this period, he would recall this Chinese poem:

紅顏離鄉白髮歸，孩童問客何處來
(Fresh-faced when one left, grey-haired upon return,
Local children ask the traveller "Where are you from?")

as well as this Japanese haiku:

furusato wa, yorumo sawarumo bara no hana.
(Nearing one's homeland is like touching a rose, beautiful but full of thorns.)

His father, having lost all of his assets in Manchuria, and now with few contacts in Taiwan, found it difficult to start a viable practice in the countryside. In these early days of their repatriation, Dr Yang's normally unquenchable confidence was severely tested. Cheng-Chao would remark to himself that they couldn't live on Dr Yang's words alone, no matter how vehement and sure the delivery. Despite the change in their circumstances, his father's authority still ruled the family. Even Cheng-Chao's younger brother,[9] who had begun to challenge his father as he entered his teens, became subdued. Seeing his father so uncertain about the family's future frightened Cheng-Chao. That their relatives seemed unwilling or unable to help further exacerbated his fear.

Not that he had much contact with his relatives. For reasons that Cheng-Chao was never able to ascertain, neither of his parents maintained close ties with their families. In a culture built on clan associations, the aloofness of their relations made the Yangs' reintegration more difficult. Cheng-Chao had been told that the Yang paternal line, like those of many Taiwanese, originated in Fujian province in the southern city of Zhangzhou. He was later to discover that his grandfather had in fact been adopted from a family surnamed Chen, about which his father knew little. Dr Yang was the fourth of six boys and three girls in the well-to-do land-owning Yang family but was the only one of the group who had attended university.

On his mother's side, Cheng-Chao knew only that she came from a prosperous Tainan family of wholesale cloth merchants. His great-grandfather had been a well-respected military man based in Kinmen, but not much is known of his origins. Though his mother spent much time gossiping at the "the well conferences"[10] of village women in Taiwanese (unlike in Manchuria where she didn't associate with the Japanese women), he didn't recall visiting or receiving many aunts, uncles, or cousins during his years in Taiwan.

The Taiwanese that he came into frequent contact with were their neighbours. In customarily blunt Taiwanese fashion, the village men and women had scornfully asked, "You can't speak Taiwanese? What kind of a Taiwanese are you?" Cheng-Chao was shamed by such comments. His parents still spoke Japanese with him and he could not learn the dialect of his ancestors at school since the language of instruction was now Mandarin. Though he eventually learned enough Taiwanese for casual conversation, he was never to completely master the tongue.

Cheng-Chao was horrified to see old women hobbling around on bound feet. He'd shuddered when his mother explained the process of breaking the bones of young girls to fit the Qing ideals of feminine beauty. It was incomprehensible to him that mangled feet could be considered an attractive trait. Even more confusing was the fact that some aged women had bound feet while others of the same era did not. It was not until he learned more about Taiwanese history that Cheng-Chao understood the diversity of the Taiwanese people.

This small island of about 36,000 square kilometres (about the size of Vancouver Island or Maryland and Delaware combined) has been home to a wide range of peoples throughout history. Located off the southeastern coast of China, the southern reach of Japan's chain of islands, and north of the Filipino archipelago, Taiwan and its surrounding smaller islands (Penghu, Matsu, and Kinmen, among others) occupy a strategic location in Southeast Asia. The native Taiwanese sometimes call themselves "sweet potatoes," referring to the yam-shaped outline of the island, to distinguish themselves from the inhabitants on the mainland of China some 180 kilometres away across the Taiwan Strait. Its geographic location makes it an important tactical point for China, a fact that has caused the island immeasurable problems in gaining international recognition as a sovereign nation.

Most archeologists believe that the first indigenous peoples settled in Taiwan from 5000 BC to 3000 BC[11] though there is archeological evidence supporting the presence of these Malayo-Polynesian aborigines dating back 15,000 years.[12] Over the millenia, several other peoples have arrived, and today there are currently sixteen official aborigine groups in Taiwan, who make up two percent of the population.[13]

Though there were visits by the Mainland Chinese prior to 1430, the first official Chinese government record of the island occurred during the Ming dynasty when the ship of a court eunuch was blown onto its shores during a storm. Throughout the fifteenth and sixteenth centuries, Chinese traders, pirates and fishermen made frequent stops on the island. Japanese pirates and traders also occasionally landed there during their expeditions. Meanwhile, numerous Hakkas, a persecuted group of Han Chinese, migrated to the island. It is estimated that a third of the Hakka population in Guangdong province immigrated to Taiwan during this time.[14]

In the late 1500s, Portuguese sailors looking for Asian trade routes popularized the name Formosa for Taiwan, reputedly derived from the exclamation made by a seaman upon seeing the spectacular scenery of Taiwan: "Ilha Formosa," beautiful island. Though the Portuguese did not manage to establish a colony on the island, the Spanish and Dutch later did. In 1662, the Dutch were driven out of Taiwan by the legendary Zheng Chenggong, also known as Koxinga, and troops loyal to the Ming emperor.

Combined with Chinese refugees fleeing famine and drought in the ensuing years, the descendants of these early Hōklo settlers comprise the largest ethnic group in Taiwan, almost seventy percent of the population. Koxinga's son continued rule for twenty years after his father's death but was eventually defeated by Qing troops in 1683. The Qing government that was subsequently established held until the surrender of Taiwan to Japan at the end of the Sino-Japanese War.

In 1946, when the Yangs first landed in Taiwan, Chiang Kai-Shek was at the beginning of what would be a fierce three-year civil war against the Communists in China. Despite billions of dollars in American aid, Chiang's Kuomintang forces were defeated. In December 1949, he fled the mainland and relocated to Taiwan. Chiang brought with him some two million Chinese mainlanders, referred to as *waishengren* (out of province people) by the locals.[15] These refugees and remnants of the Nationalist military were to spend the next four decades cut off from their homeland as the borders between Taiwan and the mainland closed.

It was into this mélange of Chinese with different origins that Cheng-Chao and his family had arrived. He eventually understood that if a woman had bound feet she was likely to be from a Hōklo family of landed gentry or aspired to marry into one. A woman with natural feet was likely to have been a servant or farm worker. Or she might be Hakka since the custom of foot-binding was forbidden among them. The practice had been banned under Japanese rule and in 1946 only a few elderly women still suffered from the pain and incapacitation of foot binding.

Aside from elders with bound feet, other unusual sights stemmed from Taiwanese religious practices. There were temples everywhere catering to Buddhist, Taoist, and Taiwanese folk religions on the island. Shrines dedicated to Matzu, Goddess of the Sea, were rampant. Considering that many of the early settlers to Taiwan had risked their lives to cross the Taiwan Strait during a time when emigration was prohibited by the Chinese government and sea voyages were treacherous, it was not surprising that the Goddess's influence lingered. But there seemed to be hundreds of other gods—mountain gods, river gods, fire gods, water gods, kitchen gods, house gods, money gods. The villagers were constantly appealing to either their ancestors or one of the myriad of gods for protection and luck.

Cheng-Chao was mystified and frightened the first time he saw a *tong ji*,[16] a Taoist spiritual medium, in action. The shaman's incomprehensible utterings and ferocious dancing left him nervous and confused. His mother later explained that the medium was supposedly in communication with a spirit and conveying messages to a relative of the departed.

Having been raised without religion other than the Shintoism dictated by the Japanese school system and to which his family did not subscribe, Cheng-Chao was puzzled by the many ways in which the Taiwanese sought answers to life decisions through divination. He couldn't understand how throwing kidney-shaped pieces of polished wood, *jiaobei* (筊杯), could foretell your future. Were the gods really conveying their wishes to the Taiwanese? Neither could he understand the other innumerable methods of divination: face-reading, palm-reading, stick-reading, star-reading. All to ensure a prosperous future. No decision, great or small, could be undertaken without consulting a geomancer. Bowing supplicants holding smoky incense sticks, tables laden with food offerings, sheaves of golden joss money tossed onto burning piles were common sights in the village.

It was during one of the religious celebrations that Cheng-Chao got his first taste of red tortoise cake (紅龜粿). He was at first unsure of the red, turtle-shaped pastry that was handed to him on a banana leaf. The shiny glutinous rice dessert looked unappetizing, but his father said that it was delicious. When Cheng-Chao bit into the soft skin and tasted the peanut filling inside, he found it only tolerable, but he could not contradict his father. If Dr Yang said a food was tasty, there was no disputing him. The pastry was served as an offering to the gods during the fast approaching Lunar New Year but he was not eager for more. The mung-bean and peanut fillings also did little for him. He much preferred Taiwanese sausages, fish balls, rice noodles, and fish. The subtropical climate of Taiwan seemed to produce a wide variety of fish; his favourite was Spanish mackerel.[17] The flora and fauna overall overwhelmed him. He'd never seen so many brilliant coloured butterflies and wild flowers. Grasshoppers, dragonflies, geckos, snails, and beetles all seemed bigger than any he'd previously encountered in Manchuria.

And there were other pleasures to experience. He enjoyed Taiwanese hand puppet theatre.[18] Painted, wooden heads mounted on elaborate cloth costumes, these puppets enacted historical sagas and traditional folk tales in open-air theatres during the festivals. The "golden light" (*jinguang* 金光) puppet shows with simple backdrops later evolved into more sophisticated programs after the introduction of television to Taiwan in 1962. In the 1970s, a series featuring the fictional character Shi Yan-wen[19] proved to be so popular that the government ordered it off the air for interfering with normal work activities. A national obsession with Little League baseball had also taken off at that time.

But Cheng-Chao had little time for diversions. As in Manchuria, his father's primary expectation for Cheng-Chao was academic excellence. No matter how desperate their finances, money for the four Yang children's school fees and uniforms could always be found. As he wolfed down his congee, Cheng-Chao mentally checked off the requirements for his school day. He'd completed his homework and made sure that he would pass the hygiene inspection. All he had to do was put on the khaki uniform with his identification number embroidered on the pocket. His father had been satisfied with Cheng-Chao's performance in the placement exam for Tainan First High School (台南一中). It was Dr Yang's own alma mater. Cheng-Chao was now in Grade Nine at the prestigious school. Had he not done well, he would have endured a terrible tongue-lashing for making his father lose face with the former classmate who was now the school vice-principal.

Cheng-Chao would later enjoy telling the story of the headmaster's son. This happened some twenty-five years after Cheng-Chao graduated, but it has an interesting lesson. Principal Lee was a severe Confucian disciplinarian who made his son practice calligraphy and study Chinese classical literature. He ran a strict academic establishment and despite crowded conditions managed to maintain the school's high standards and good reputation. Graduates of the school often scored well enough on the university entrance exams to enter the top educational institution in the country, National Taiwan University. To Principal Lee's great disappointment, his son twice failed the exams. Furthermore, the young man decided to enroll in a theatre school after graduation, the equivalent of joining the circus in a country that looked down on performers in general. That disappointing son was Oscar-winning director Ang Lee.

Cheng-Chao's father expected him to reach the upper reaches of society through education. In the ancient class-tiered system, *shi-nong-gong-shàng* (士農工商), Dr Yang expected his children to become the gentry-scholars of the top *shi* tier and not the farmers, craftsmen or merchants of the lower orders. As Cheng-Chao pulled on the long tan pants, white socks, and canvas shoes that were part of his school uniform, he felt the pressure of his father's expectations. Though he was a good student, he would have to compensate for his complete lack of knowledge of Chinese in order to succeed.

Bidding farewell to his parents, Cheng-Chao walked the twenty minutes to Yongkang train station. He saw housewives hanging out laundry on bamboo clotheslines and uniformed schoolchildren with schoolbags slung over their shoulders as he plodded along the dirt-paved roads of the sleepy town. Since Yongkang was the last station before the terminus stop, Tainan City, the train would invariably be packed by the time it pulled in to the station. After the orderly life to which he had become accustomed in Manchuria, the rough jostling of train passengers as they swarmed the doors often made him nervous. He had watched aghast the first time he saw a man pulled through a window into a moving train. Did these things happen when the Japanese ruled? He was a stranger in his native land, and he would have to adapt.

White Terror

It was the first day of classes and the classroom was atwitter with speculations about Teacher Wang. Some students said he was merely sick. Some said he had been "disappeared" by the government. Some even said he had been killed, like his brother—yet another intellectual to be executed by the KMT.

Teacher Wang[1] was one of a small handful of Taiwanese instructors employed at the school. A scholar in the Hokkien dialect, Teacher Wang taught Chinese history to the upper level boys. Wang's engaging stories had ignited an interest in history in quite a few students. He was Cheng-Chao's favourite teacher, and to the seventeen-year-old's mind, one of the few role models on the staff.

The rest of the teachers were Mainlanders who had arrived with the Kuomintang. Charged with converting the Taiwanese "Japanese slaves" into loyal Chinese subjects fluent in Mandarin, these teachers spoke with a variety of accents. Those from Beijing laid claim to the most superior brand of Mandarin, the standard Chinese of the ruling elite from the Qing dynasty, and looked down on the teachers from the other cities and provinces. Cheng-Chao found the accents confusing. He would learn what he thought was the proper pronunciation of a word from one teacher only to be corrected by the next. His classmates were also in the same position. Having been educated entirely in the Japanese school system prior to 1945, they were more fluent in Japanese than Taiwanese. Fortunately for Cheng-Chao, this made it easier for him to downplay his deficiency in Taiwanese at school.

In the transition from Japanese to Chinese rule, Mandarin had become the official language and Japanese usage in newspapers was abolished in 1946.[2] Mandarin cram schools proliferated overnight as men and women sped to learn the language in order to earn a living and negotiate the Chinese bureaucracy. Native Taiwanese who were not fluent in Mandarin could not even think of working for the government. However, with or without the proper language skills, thousands of Taiwanese civil servants had been displaced by Mainlanders. If that were not enough, the 100,000 Taiwanese who had returned from abroad after the war competed with locals and Mainlanders for jobs.[3] Mainlander officials took this opportunity to avail themselves of plum jobs. Chen Yi, Chiang Kai-Shek's Administrator General of Taiwan, ran the island so much to his own nepotistic benefit that his government had been nicknamed Chen Yi Enterprises Unlimited by the locals.[4] The 30,000 Mainlanders who arrived with Chen Yi looted the countryside so thoroughly that Taiwan faced a rice shortage for the first time in its history.[5]

Naturally, this did not sit well with the descendants of peoples with a history of resistance. Even under Qing rule, Taiwan was a troublesome spot for the Manchu emperors—an outlying island where there was "trouble every three years, chaos every five."[6] At the time of the Japanese takeover, the locals declared a short-lived Republic of Taiwan and fought a guerilla war for three years against superior Japanese weaponry. After the "pacification" of the island, the Taiwanese continued to fight using political means, though occasional uprisings such as the 1915 Tainan incident continued.[7] Taiwanese home rule movements sprang up despite Japanese assimilationist policies and education. The desire of the Taiwanese to have a voice in their own government during the fifty years of colonization had yielded small gains.[8] With the arrival of the Chinese, it seemed as though the Taiwanese had been returned to colonial rule.

Though Cheng-Chao had little knowledge of Taiwan before his return, the strength of the villagers in their Taiwanese identity was evident to him from the start. His parents, like the other villagers, referred to Tainan City with pride as Fushia, the prefecture city. The oldest city in Taiwan, Tainan had served as the administrative centre for so many regimes that it was nicknamed the "phoenix city." Its stints under the Dutch, Chinese, and Japanese left a rich legacy of temples, government buildings, and monuments. The fine arts of Chinese culture such as music, painting, and calligraphy had thrived. Folk traditions, exemplified by Taoist and Buddhist rites, were still practiced by the common folk.

But in 1947, Tainan's history took a bloody turn, with an incident that has come to exemplify the brutality of Kuomintang rule. It began in the north of Taiwan. On February 27, inspectors from the newly established Monopoly Bureau confronted a forty-year-old widow named Lin Chiang-mai and her young daughter for selling contraband cigarettes in Taipei. A small crowd gathered as the woman pleaded for the return of the confiscated cigarettes and money. One of the agents struck her on the head with his pistol causing her to bleed from the gash and the crowd became incensed. In making their escape, one of the agents accidentally fired upon a bystander who later died. The crowd burned the Monopoly Bureau vehicle but the agents managed to find refuge in a nearby police station.[9]

The following morning, in what is now known as the notorious

2-2-8 Incident, a crowd of demonstrators took to the streets beating
gongs and drums. They marched from Taipei Park to the Monopoly
Bureau headquarters with placards and a petition demanding justice.
When they got no response from the Bureau, the now two-thou-
sand-strong crowd made their way to Chen Yi's office. There, they
faced soldiers who had been dispatched to protect the Executive
Office. Without warning, a machine gun on the building rooftop
fired upon the crowd killing two and injuring several others. The
maddened throng spread out into the surrounding streets and set
upon any Mainlanders they encountered. The crowds beat up the
staff of the Monopoly Bureau and ransacked the building, smash-
ing windows and burning papers. Young men with Japanese military training disarmed the local police officers and took over several
police stations.[10] On the evening of February 28, Chen Yi's Garrison
Command declared martial law and military patrols took over Taipei,
firing indiscriminately upon people on the streets.[11]

Pent-up anger and frustration against the government burst
forth when news of the Taipei incidents spread. Within two days,
an island-wide protest was underway and riots ensued in the cities
and countryside. Chen Yi was faced with the problem of quelling the
insurrection with insufficient troops. In March 1947, the Chinese
civil war was entering its final phase of heavy fighting, especially in
Manchuria and northeastern China, where the Communists were
gaining ground. The number of soldiers in Taiwan had been reduced
from 48,000 to 11,000 as the Nationalists steadily lost ground and
men were dispatched to active battle.[12] In order to buy time as he
waited for reinforcements from the mainland, Chen agreed to
negotiations with a hastily formed Taiwanese delegation composed
of prominent businessmen and professionals. On March 1, the
Settlement Committee requested compensation for the victims of
2-2-8 and punishment of the police involved in the initial incidents
as well as the lifting of martial law.[13] Chen made a radio broadcast

agreeing to restitution for victims and amnesty for the Taiwanese who had been arrested. On March 7, the Committee presented him with a proposal for political and economic reform[14] which would give the Taiwanese more autonomy in their own government. Chen angrily rejected the list and the Committee retreated to alter the proposal. On March 8, 13,000 Nationalist soldiers landed on Taiwan.[15]

The troops that arrived at the ports carried out a bloody massacre along the western coastal cities of Taiwan over the next few days. One of Chen Yi's bodyguards said years later that Chiang Kai-Shek had sent a telegram to Chen instructing him to "Kill them all; keep it secret."[16] The worst violence occurred in Keelung and Kaohsiung where the troops first landed as well as in Taipei and Chiayi. KMT troops fired indiscriminately at the shores even before the ships docked. In Keelung, soldiers went into action as soon as they landed: raping, bayoneting, robbing, and looting. Some victims were stuffed into burlap bags, chained, or tied with wires and thrown alive into the sea.[17] Truckloads of bodies were dumped into nearby waterways. Keelung Harbour and Taipei's Tamsui River turned red with bloodied, rotting corpses.[18]

Targeted attacks of prominent locals from a previously compiled blacklist were systematically carried out. Journalists, educators, students, lawyers, politicians, and any who had criticized the government or could provide leadership such as the members of the Settlement Committee were all vulnerable. Men were dragged from their homes and shot immediately or killed later as a warning to others. Family members were forced to watch as public executions were carried out. In Kaohsiung, local citizens who had gathered in an auditorium to discuss the crisis were strafed with machine guns after the doors were sealed.[19] Many victims were tortured and mutilated before their corpses were left on the streets, again as a grim warning to the rest of the population.[20]

By March 13, the major cities had been "pacified," and the entire island was under strict government control by the end of the month, as Operation Countryside Cleanup concluded.[21] All told, at least 10,000 Taiwanese were killed or went missing during this time.[22] Some estimates say the number killed was as high as 28,000.[23] By eliminating the local educated elite and creating a leadership vacuum in the major centres, the Nationalists hoped to prevent future uprisings. They were to repeat the process of targeted police searches, arrests, and executions in 1949-51. Taiwanese activists advocating for democracy were forced to flee the country if they managed to survive the purges.[24]

The intellectuals in Tainan were not spared in the initial sweep. Cheng-Chao felt a sense of foreboding about Teacher Wang's disappearance. He knew that Teacher Wang's brother[25] had been one of the victims of the 2-2-8 purge. Educated as a lawyer at Tokyo Imperial University, he had been working in Taipei. His was one of the many corpses thrown into the Tamsui River in the first killings. But it was the death of another Tainan native that had the greatest impact on Cheng-Chao's life. Though they did not often discuss politics at home, Cheng-Chao's father had impressed upon him the gravity of the political situation after Dr Yang experienced a traumatic incident.

In March 1947, Dr Yang witnessed the execution of Tang De-jhang in the park fronting Tainan City Hall.[26] Born of a Japanese father and Taiwanese mother and trained as a lawyer in Japan before returning to Taiwan in 1943, forty-year-old Tang had been a popular candidate for the mayor of Tainan. He served as chairman of the Tainan People's Freedom Protection Committee and negotiated with the authorities during 2-2-8. When the military asked for a list of participants in the uprising, Tang refused. Falsely accused as a separatist, he had apparently been tortured then paraded around the city with a placard on his back before arriving at the park. Defiant to the last, Tang refused to kneel before his executioners. He was shot through the head, and his family not allowed to collect his corpse for several days.[27]

On the evening of the execution, Dr Yang came home ashen-faced and gathered his children around him after dinner.

"Don't ever get involved with politics! Do you understand?"

Cheng-Chao and his siblings nodded gravely, frightened by their father's agitated manner. It was only later, after the shock of the execution had subsided that Dr Yang enlightened his children regarding his edict. In the years following, Dr Yang was to repeat the same warning multiple times as the climate of fear prevailed. There would be many friends and acquaintances who would suddenly disappear overnight in the thirty-eight years of martial law that was imposed.

Though the comparatively moderate Wei Tao-Ming had replaced Governor General Chen Yi and lifted martial law for a short time, the arrival of Chiang Kai-Shek in December 1949 after his rout in the Chinese civil war ended the brief respite from military rule.[28] As early as 1948, Chiang had begun preparing for a retreat to Taiwan, when defeat seemed imminent. Instead of importing food and goods from the island to support the war effort as in years prior, he ordered the secret removal of China's gold reserves and most of the contents of Beijing's National Palace Museum to the island as well as the rebuilding of Taiwan's economy. KMT supporters began to flee to the last safe haven available and, including 600,000 members of the Nationalist army, had raised the population of Taiwan by about two million after the civil war was lost in 1949.[29]

As well as refugees, Chiang also brought with him the political apparatus of the mainland. The Chinese constitution had been written in 1946, without Communist participation, for a nation that included all of China and Outer Mongolia.[30] Chiang was elected president in 1948. The last legislative elections also took place that year and all the "representatives" of China now held their seats as they settled in Taiwan. Chiang himself resumed his presidency in March 1950 (after having "retired" in January 1949 while the war was going badly).[31] As a result, a Taiwanese population of no more than ten million supported a parliament of two thousand members originally chosen to govern several hundred million on the mainland.[32] Until well into the 1980s, Chiang, and later his son, Chiang Ching-Kuo, maintained a *de facto* one-party system dominated by the Mainlanders. The older Chiang had his parliament remove restrictions on the number of terms that a President could serve to ensure that he could rule for life.[33] Although local elections were allowed, few Taiwanese were able to compete against KMT candidates backed by the government's enormous coffers and organizational apparatus to gain a foothold on power at the national level. Furthermore, in 1954, the Council of Grand Justices declared that the winners of the last mainland national elections would sit until voting could again take place on the mainland. As these elected members died, they were replaced with the second and even third place losers of the 1947-48 mainland elections.[34]

Using the pretext of suppressing "Communist bandits" to consolidate his power on the island, Chiang had ordered the Governor of Taiwan to declare martial law in May 1949.[35] Chiang was accustomed to treating Communists harshly and had taken every opportunity to eliminate them on the mainland. When the Americans created the Sino-American Cooperative Organization in 1943 to coordinate Allied offensives against the Japanese in China, Chiang assigned the head of his secret police, Tai Li, to the task. Aside from being the KMT teaching facility for 50,000 anti-Japanese guerillas, many of the fourteen training camps housed prisons, complete with torture chambers, where Communists were taken. Despite American objections, Chiang's private army, funded by the United States, continued to operate these camps and target Communists until the People's Liberation Army arrived at the end of the civil war.[36] It was with this mindset that Chiang governed Taiwan. Thus began the White Terror, the longest period of martial law in the history of the modern world.[37]

In fact, the Communist movement was ineffectual and of little consequence in Taiwan. Before 2-2-8, the Chinese Communist Party (CCP) had only about seventy recruits in Taiwan. The bloody crackdown by the KMT boosted CCP ranks to 300 by the end of 1947 as disenchanted Taiwanese sought a way of protesting against the Nationalists.[38] In Taipei, the CCP's Taiwan Province Work Committee, comprised mostly of bus drivers and postal workers, staged one strike and one demonstration in 1948-49. At its peak in 1950, there were only about 900 members and the organization quickly collapsed when some of its leaders gave themselves up and divulged information to the KMT that led to massive arrests of the membership.[39]

Nevertheless, in the 1950s, most of the KMT's prosecutions were of Mainlanders and Taiwanese engaged in alleged Communist activities. In 1950, the Legislative Yuan passed an amendment to the 1949 "Traitors Punishment Act," which decreed a death punishment for insurrection.[40] Furthermore, accusers stood to profit from inform-ing. Successful prosecutions of "banditry and espionage" cases netted informants and prosecutors shares in the confiscated properties.[41]

During this time, many unwary intellectuals were charged with sedition and arrested for belonging to discussion groups or writing for independent publications.[42] Regardless of guilt or innocence, a mere accusation was often sufficient to significantly alter people's lives. Chiang Ching-Kuo, head of the KMT secret police, would eventually create the National Security Bureau, which employed 50,000 full-time and half a million part-time informants by the late 1960s.[43] A culture of self-censorship had developed. The KMT thus became universally hated and feared by the Taiwanese. But still, to hold a job one often had to join the KMT, which Cheng-Chao's father did for a short time, to his everlasting shame afterwards.

By the 1960s, KMT focus had changed from hunting Communist spies to arresting Taiwanese democracy advocates. In 1948, at the height of the civil war, the National Assembly had banned the formation of new political parties with the expectation that civil liberties and democratic principles would be restored after the Communists were defeated.[44] After the KMT defeat in 1949, these and other provisions, which gave Chiang sweeping powers over government, were maintained indefinitely. Anyone who dared to criticize the KMT or push for political reform was arrested as a traitor and taken to Taipei. Confessions extracted through torture at local police stations or military garrisons were frequently admitted as evidence during these sham trials. Political prisoners were sent to the notorious Green Island or other prisons for decades, if they were not sentenced to death.[45] Family members of the political dissidents were often harassed and put under surveillance. Those who had served out their sentences frequently found that their properties had been seized and their job prospects were greatly diminished. The stories of suffering were innumerable. Conservative estimates place the number of political trials at over 2,900 and the number of executions during the White Terror at three to four thousand;[46] other estimates put the number of trials closer to 10,000 and those summarily executed to as high as 45,000.[47]

The government had also begun to isolate the islanders and control information. In April 1950, tourism and even visits abroad were banned. Radio sets were registered and newspapers and letters censored.[48] Even foreign publications, such as *Time* magazine, were "sanitized."

The KMT also sought to eradicate local language and culture and replace it with Chinese practices. Missionaries were not allowed to preach in Hōklo, Hakka or aboriginal languages. Folk religions went underground. Music played on radio stations had to be "sanitized" and the number of hours of television programming in local dialects were severely restricted, going down to as low as one hour per day in 1972.[49]

Just as Mao was doing on the mainland, Chiang was aiming to rule via a cult of personality. Starting in 1950, he set about manufacturing a culture of deification. Streets, schools, and parks were named after him; statues and pictures of him began appearing on school campuses; and his sayings became part of the required curriculum. He was cast as the ultimate Confucian patriarch—a sage for the people.[50] Posters and billboards exhorted citizens to reunify China. Radio and television spots cautioned the people against the Communist threat.[51] A large portion of the national budget, some claim over fifty percent, was allocated to the military.[52] Compulsory basic military training for young men over age eighteen was introduced and continues to this day.

In reality, the odds favoured the Chinese Communist Party (CCP), had there been a conflict. The Truman administration officially cut off military aid to the Kuomintang at the start of 1950. At the same time, the Sino-Soviet alliance was growing stronger. British and American analysts predicted that the Communists would take the island by the summer of 1950. Then fate intervened in the form of the Korean War. Fearful of the spread of Soviet and Chinese Communism in the region, Truman ordered the Seventh Fleet to protect the "unsinkable aircraft carrier" that was Taiwan. American forces protected the island from CCP attack throughout the Cold War, securing Chiang's place on the island and giving him the liberty to pursue his agenda of complete domination over Taiwan while maintaining the façade of running "Free China."[53]

Cheng-Chao would spend his entire educational career in Taiwan bowing to large portraits of President Chiang in his classrooms, being inundated with government slogans such as "It is everyone's duty to report Communist spies," and reading government-censored textbooks depicting Chiang as a great hero.[54] None of the books contained Taiwanese history; the only history worthy of study was that of China's. Students were punished for speaking Taiwanese dialects among themselves and anyone who spoke Mandarin with a Taiwanese accent was disparaged. Just as in Manchuria, Cheng-Chao again felt inferior; this time, to the Mainlanders.

After Teacher Wang's disappearance, Cheng-Chao tried to glean as much information about him as he could but there was no news of him. Months later he heard with great relief that Wang had flown to Hong Kong then made his way to Japan. He and his wife had left on July 4, the first day of summer vacation. They were now established in Tokyo, where Wang was preparing to resume his studies. He would eventually earn a doctorate from the University of Tokyo. Cheng-Chao would learn of his former teacher's address in Japan a decade later; the link would prompt him to forever disregard his father's prohibitions against political involvement.

Transformation

In an era when arranged marriages were still the norm and dating was frowned upon, twenty-three-year-old Cheng-Chao found himself sitting across from a woman who called herself Jane, in a booth at the Tianma Café.[1] Her Chinese name was Wang Ai-chen. He had first met her in 1951, when he was in his second year of pre-medical studies at National Taiwan University (Taida). The 2-2-8 incident had begun right outside the building where they sat now, though Cheng-Chao's thoughts were not on the historical significance of the spot he had picked. He had finally saved up enough money to take a girl out on a real date. It was fortunate that both their families were in Tainan, while they were left to fend for themselves in the north, a freedom afforded few young couples in Asia at the time.

When the university entrance examination results were announced, his name had not been on the bulletin boards displaying the *Zhonghua ribao* pages listing the successful candidates.[2] It seemed that he would have to sit for the exams for Taida again the following year, or study engineering, agriculture, or teaching at one of the colleges. More than ten of his classmates, many with decidedly lower school marks, had been successful. Cheng-Chao ran to check the rival paper. To his great relief, he found his name there. He immediately bought a copy and brought it home, knowing his father would have read the *Zhonghua ribao* at work. Upon arrival at home, his brother, Cheng-Yi (Tadahisa), hopped on his bicycle and delivered the purchased newspaper to their father's clinic. It was only after reading the second paper that Dr Yang's sour mood lightened into a proud smile.

But at the end of the first year, Cheng-Chao decided to quit medical school.

When he announced his decision at home, the scene in the living room unfolded exactly as he feared it would.

"But why do you want to quit? You got in. Pre-med guarantees you a medical career. Why do you want to give that up?" Dr Yang yelled.

"Because I don't have a lot in common with the other students. They think just because they're going to be doctors, they're better than anyone else," Cheng-Chao replied.

He frequently recalled the Japanese proverb: *Noo aru taka wa, tsume o kakusu.* (The talented hawk hides its claws; i.e. "still waters run deep.")

"There is no way you're going to quit medicine. You're going to be a doctor and that's final."

The tension persisted in the house despite his mother's attempts to mediate. Finally, a thoroughly cowed Cheng-Chao returned to Taipei to continue his medical studies. He would later appreciate his father's wisdom and understand the folly of his naiveté and immaturity. Now, only three more years remained of the seven-year program and though his opinion about his classmates had not changed, he had learned mostly to ignore them. He had few intimate friends.

That was why he cherished Jane all the more.

Jane's entry into his life was one machination of his father's to which Cheng-Chao did not object. In 1951, Jane was enrolled as a first-year zoology student at Taida, a program for which she found no liking. She had done badly in chemistry during the first term so her father, Dr Wang,[3] set about engaging a tutor for her. He turned to his friend, Dr Yang, for help. The two physicians had been schoolmates at medical school and both had lived in Manchuria until the end of the war. Dr Wang and Dr Yang conferred and Cheng-Chao was chosen as the tutor.

Though Jane and Cheng-Chao had been in Manchuria at the same time, they'd lived in different cities. Jane's maternal grandfather, Dr Chen,[4] an early pioneer in Manchuria, had been wealthy, owning several apple orchards and vegetable farms. He also operated a charitable hospital in Dalian.[5] His wife had been one of the first Japanese-trained Taiwanese midwives in the Japanese Empire and had been invited to visit the Empress, a real honour. Like most Taiwanese repatriates from Manchuria, the Wangs had left most of their belongings behind when they fled.

Cheng-Chao found Jane to be the most *yasashii* person he had met, a gentle and kind soul. She had the keys to a zoology classroom in the science building and that was where the lessons took place. They slowly worked through Linus Pauling's chemistry textbook. They spent many evenings talking and getting to know each other. After passing her chemistry course, she'd switched her major to Foreign Literature, specializing in Jane Austen. But they had continued their association.

They braved mosquitoes as they strolled the palm tree-lined boulevards of the campus and ducked under the arched walkways in between the 1920s Japanese-style buildings. They studied next to each other in the library at the reading desks. He was acutely conscious of her as she spun her green leather chair to reach for her books in her bag. He tried to keep his own reading chair steady on its wooden base as he concentrated on his medical books, resisting the urge to flick on the switch of the her desk lamp so he could better see her. He made the daily trek across campus from the No. 8 men's dormitory to the women's dormitory. She was so different from anyone Cheng-Chao had ever encountered before. He thought her Chinese name particularly fitting—Wang Ai-chen—lover of truth.[6]

Jane once told him about her childhood illness in Manchuria. Born in Dalian in 1932, she had contracted what was likely post-measles pneumonia when she was three. All the physicians concurred that she was beyond help and would never survive. The family had arranged for a child-sized casket in preparation for the inevitable. Her father, though, had continued to minister to her in stubborn persistence. And she made a miraculous recovery and became grateful for her life ever since. Each day was a gift from God. She was even considering becoming a missionary like some of the teachers she'd met in the mission high school. She came by her religion naturally; in addition to her childhood experience, Jane's paternal grandfather had been a Presbyterian preacher. Reverend Wang had been one of the early Christian converts in Taiwan and the family still followed the faith.

At the time of Reverend Wang's conversion, Asia had long been an attractive destination for Western missionaries who wished to bring the "heathen" to Christ. Catholics, Protestants, and other groups sent devout men and women to Asia from Canada, the United States, and Great Britain throughout the nineteenth century. Before this onslaught, the Chinese had already been exposed to Christianity in the late sixteenth century when Jesuit priest Matteo Ricci ingratiated himself with Emperor Wanli by introducing Western culture, science, and mathematics to the Ming imperial court. As China was pried open by Western nations during the trade wars of the mid to late 1800s, more and more missionaries gained admission into the country. By the 1930s, missionaries from a diverse range of Christian denominations could be found throughout China. Aside from Catholic and Protestant missionaries, there were Mormons, Jehovah's Witnesses, and Russian Orthodox followers. Belgian Benedictines could be found in Sichuan, German Augustines in Shanghai, Swiss Canons Regular of Grand St Bernard in Tibet, and a bewildering host of other Christian sects in every reach of the Chinese empire.[7]

In the north of Taiwan, one lone missionary from the Canadian Presbyterian Church stands out. George Lesley Mackay became a well-known name to Cheng-Chao and a life-long influence, though the two never met. Born in Oxford County, Ontario in 1844 to Highland Scots who had emigrated after the Sutherland Clearances, Mackay was brought up in a pious Presbyterian household. The youngest of six children, he was called to mission early in his life. Upon completion of his Presbyterian education,[8] he sailed as the first Canadian missionary to China in 1872. He chose northern Taiwan as his parish and began a remarkable thirty-year career.

A small man in a grey suit, known to the locals as the "black-bearded barbarian," he was pelted with mud and debris as he tried to evangelize in front of Taiwanese temples. But Mackay mastered the Taiwanese language and was able to preach in open-air temples and argue with the local literati schooled in the Chinese classics regarding religion and philosophy within five months of landing. His first convert was a young Confucian scholar named Giam Cheng-Hao, who had led several groups of Chinese intellectuals to Mackay in anticipation of debunking the missionary's beliefs but ended up being won over by Mackay's arguments.[9]

Mackay's interests were wide-ranging. His book, *From Far Formosa*, detailed the island's geography, history, geology, flora and fauna, religion, and ethnology like no other before. Some of his collection of Taiwan's cultural artifacts is housed at Toronto's Royal Ontario Museum. He spent much time evangelizing among the aboriginal peoples in eastern Taiwan and was one of the foremost experts of his time on native culture. He is credited with introducing carrots, tomatoes, and cauliflowers to the island.[10] He is also known for establishing the first western medical clinic in northern Taiwan, a girls' school,[11] the country's oldest western-style university,[12] and the first Taiwanese museum.[13] His "sermons" were not confined to Bible study but took in topics as diverse as astronomy, anatomy, physiology, and geography. Despite his lack of formal training, he would regularly practice medicine and dentistry among potential converts. His "services" were mixtures of song, sermon, and healing.[14]

Though his methods and some of his ideas were controversial, Mackay was elected Moderator of the Canadian Presbyterian Church in 1894. As Moderator, he spoke out against the Chinese head tax, calling it racist. He questioned the effectiveness of female foreign missionaries in Taiwan, advocating instead for the recruitment of local women. Despite some of his unpopular views, Mackay's mission became the fastest growing in Asia, and donations poured in from Canada. He was able to finance the construction of a boys' school called Oxford College (now Aletheia University), as well as Mackay Clinic (named after a Detroit shipping captain, who was no relation).[15] In 1911, a few years after his death, the clinic was renamed the Mackay Memorial Hospital and moved to Taipei from Tamsui.

In his old age, Cheng-Chao would visit Zorra, the town in southern Ontario where Mackay was born and raised. He would marvel that one small church could produce almost forty ministers and the phenomenon that was Mackay. He would also ruminate on the question of identity that had plagued him his entire life and remark that missionaries like Mackay were in fact more Taiwanese than he. They had spent most of their lives in Taiwan and had chosen their new homes willingly. That Mackay had married a native Taiwanese woman, Zhang Cong-ming,[16] in part to become more integrated into local life and in part to attract women to the faith, spoke not only to his devotion to mission but also to his identification with the Taiwanese. Mackay "went native" more than any other missionary of the time, a decision that caused great controversy in Canada. He is the only missionary mentioned in Taiwanese textbooks and the only one honoured with a commemorative stamp.[17] In a country dominated by Chinese religions, that Mackay is revered as a national hero speaks to how much the Taiwanese appreciate his contributions and his intimate link with the people.

However, in the 1950s, as the KMT consolidated its control over the island, it increasingly targeted Christians and other religious groups. Ironically, Chiang Kai-Shek's wife, Soong Mei-Ling, was the daughter of Charlie Soong, a Methodist missionary who had amassed a fortune printing Bibles for Western missionaries; and she was herself a Christian. Madame Chiang was also the sister-in-law of Sun Yat-Sen, the Congregationalist revolutionary who had toppled the Manchus and is revered as the father of modern China. Fluent in English, Madame Chiang's tour of Christian America during the Second World War had greatly bolstered the popularity of the Kuomintang in the United States. Nevertheless, starting in 1957, all missionaries were prohibited from preaching in local dialects.[18] In 1959, Yiguandao[19] members were put under surveillance and the sect was forced to disband and go underground. In 1963, the influential Japanese Buddhist Nichiren sect was compelled to dissolve. Government harassment of religious adherents continued well into the 1970s and 80s.[20]

A Catholic nun was Cheng-Chao's first white teacher. Her gentle, kind, but strict handling of the freshman class was a novelty for him after the Chinese English teachers he'd encountered during his high school years. He'd been selected for her class on the basis of his entrance examination marks. When he sat the exams, there'd only been four subjects: math, science, English, and Chinese. The math test had been so difficult that year that two-thirds of the candidates had received zero. Cheng-Chao was proud to have achieved 33% in the test. When it came to Chinese, though, he thought it would have been easier to start counting his ranking from the bottom of the heap.

Cheng-Chao could not later recall whether the sister had tried to convert him. He rarely attended church services during his university years. Though Jane was a devout churchgoer, she did not insist on his accompanying her. It was enough for him to be able to see her regularly. In his third year, since classes such as anatomy, physiology, and pharmacology now took place at the medical school near the Taipei train station, he'd moved to the dormitories there. As often as he could, he'd take the bus back to the main campus and wait among the mostly overseas students at the counter of the girls' dormitory while Jane was called down. He and Jane would then set off for their walks around campus. He was content with life, especially now that he was finally getting to see patients. He hoped to become a good doctor.

For Cheng-Chao, Jane was the love of his life, his first and last girlfriend. Her sense of humility and gratitude made him a better man and was the single greatest influence on his character. They would marry in a Western-style church ceremony in February 1957. Their first child, Mark, would be born late that year and their first daughter, Nancy, two years later.

But the young family was not destined to make their life in Taiwan. Aside from the repressive rule of the Kuomintang government and the resultant restrictions on free speech, Cheng-Chao and his new bride bristled at the prevailing social customs. Though husband and wife assumed traditional roles in the division of domestic labour, Cheng-Chao believed in women's rights, and that may have been a factor in his choosing gynecology and obstetrics as his specialty. The Confucian custom of favouring boys over girls[21] had seen Jane's mother rushing to Taipei to check the outcome of her daughter's first pregnancy. Mrs Wang wanted to ensure that her daughter had support in case the child was a girl. Fortunately, Jane had done her duty on the first try and Mrs Wang was able to return to Tainan with an easy mind.

Cheng-Chao and Jane were also handicapped by their lack of social connections. In a society built on *guanxi*,[22] Manchurian-Taiwanese repatriates such as the Yangs and Wangs lacked the social and business connections that those who had never left the island enjoyed. Though, after Mark's birth, Jane was able to secure a teaching job in Taipei with her uncle's help, future prospects for the Yangs were limited. Chiang Kai-Shek's totalitarian rule was prompting many educated young Taiwanese to seek a way out of the country. In 1959, while Jane was pregnant with their second child, Cheng-Chao left his family behind in search of a brighter future and forever changed their fortunes.

Part III

North America
1959–present
Charles Yang

· 9 ·

Culture Shock Again

DETROIT, 1962

The haggard-looking black woman had been in labour for hours. As with most of the patients that Charles Yang saw at Detroit's Herman Kiefer Hospital, he'd not had contact with her prior to her delivery. He was now in the second year of his four-year residency in gynecology and obstetrics, and he had become accustomed to the daily stream of patients. The hospital delivered almost six thousand babies a year, an average of sixteen per day. While most deliveries were performed by interns under the supervision of residents, Charles, a junior resident, was responsible for at least a couple of the more complicated deliveries each day. He was thankful for the experience since it helped him hone his skills; unlike the limits placed on interns when he was in Chicago. But this promised to be a difficult delivery and Charles was glad the chief resident would be supervising. A quick examination had revealed two small feet right at the vaginal opening. An undiagnosed breech. He quickly administered an epidural.

This was the thirty-five-year-old mother's sixth pregnancy—another multipara patient who had not received prenatal care and was delivering without family support. Technically, the woman should be called a grand multipara, with the number of children she had already borne. The preponderance of unwed mothers on welfare with numerous young children surprised him. Charles couldn't fathom why people who were poor persisted in perpetuating the cycle for their children and why it seemed socially acceptable to do so. After he became better acquainted with North American society, Charles would gradually begin to understand Western ways, but during his early days in the new country, many customs baffled him.

Charles was reeling from culture shock. In 1959, he had left twenty-seven-year-old Jane in Taipei, pregnant with their second child, and embarked on his first plane trip, flying from Taiwan to San Francisco with stops in Midway, Guam, and Hawaii, finally landing in Chicago to begin an internship at $50 per month with Mount Sinai Hospital. It was a lonely year. He missed Jane and two-year-old Mark terribly. He was given room and board at the hospital and spent almost all his time there working or improving his language skills. He had been so cloistered that he'd not even known there was a Chinatown in the city until near the end of his stay, when he tasted Chinese food for the first time in nearly a year. By then, he'd become accustomed to the kosher food served in the hospital cafeteria: the salads, the lack of pork, the unleavened breads. He was now also less overwhelmed by vehicle traffic and large buildings. The sights and sounds of Chicago—skyscrapers towering above him and express-ways humming with vehicles racing along at crazy speeds—had dumbfounded him after the sedate pace of Taipei with its quiet roads.

He'd begun the Detroit residency in 1960 at a more livable wage of $300 per month. Using his monies from Taiwan and what he could save from his salary, Charles managed to accumulate $2400 in the bank in order to satisfy immigration regulations for sponsoring his family. After extensive Taiwanese bureaucracy that included tests for tuberculosis and numerous visits to government offices for interviews, exit permits for his wife and children were granted.

On September 23, 1962, Charles had planned to meet Jane and the two children at the airport after his shift. He'd spoken with Jane only a few times during the three years. Overseas calls were expensive and their conversations over the phone lines within earshot of others had been awkward and were stilted. Feelings were better expressed through writing. He had not yet seen his two-year-old daughter, Nancy, and the anticipation was unbearable.

After a delay in San Francisco, his family finally arrived. They rented a one-bedroom apartment on Fairview Street for $35 a month. A Murphy bed in the living room doubled as a second bedroom. They attended Jefferson Presbyterian Church and were warmly welcomed by Reverend and Mrs Thompson, with whom they spent their first Thanksgiving. It was the first but not the last time that their Christian beliefs would ease the Yangs' route to assimilation.

Integration would prove more difficult for the three Japanese physicians who lived in their apartment building. Wartime propaganda in America had been so effective that hatred toward Germans and Japanese still lingered. Often, they noticed, when people found out that the Yangs were not Japanese, a thaw in attitudes would occur. But Jane befriended the wives of the Japanese doctors, finding solace in speaking the tongue of her childhood and camaraderie in the shared chores of raising young children. It was comforting to be with women who also knew the meaning of 廃物利用.[1] The frugality inculcated in the Yangs during Taiwan's austerity period was now a fundamental part of their characters, and would remain a lifelong habit regardless of their later circumstances. They had both been amazed by the wasteful habits of Americans and the abundance of everything.

Aside from the Japanese doctors and their wives, the Yangs

generally socialized only with the few expatriates in the area who were Taiwanese and among the first to leave the island. Most of these adventurous souls were male exchange students pursuing advanced degrees. The Taiwanese government allowed studies abroad only if the students had served two to three years of compulsory military service.[2] Most of them had also sat government exams to ensure their fitness to represent the country before they were granted permission to leave.[3] Because of his severe myopia, Charles had been exempted from conscription and, astonishingly, he had also obtained a five-year exchange visa without complications after his offer of employment arrived from Mount Sinai Hospital in Chicago.

Though there was a small Chinatown in Detroit's Cass Corridor, Charles and the Taiwanese students found little in common with its inhabitants. Descendants of early immigrants to the United States, the American-born Chinese usually spoke Cantonese and not the Hakka or Hokkien/Hōklo dialects of the native Taiwanese, the *benshengren*.[4] They also did not identify with the recent Mandarin-speaking immigrants from China who had briefly lived in Taiwan before escaping to America. To them, these *waishengren*,[5] many of them KMT bureaucrats and their relatives or wealthy businessmen from China, represented the government that was oppressing their families in Taiwan.

Most of these Taiwanese students would remain in the United States after completing their degrees, beginning the brain drain from Taiwan in the decades after 1949. In contrast to the years prior, when students most often studied in Japan or England, America became a favourite destination for Taiwanese students, especially after the 1965 Immigration Reform Act[6] in the US increased the quota of ethnic Chinese immigrants to 20,000 per year. An average of 2000 students per year arrived from Taiwan through the 1960s and 70s. But in 1962-63, when the Yangs were in Detroit, there were only about 2000 Taiwanese students abroad worldwide.[7] Those studying in the United States were mostly concentrated on the east and west coasts with a small group in Chicago. The number in Detroit was miniscule and, as a man with a family, Charles tried to include as many bachelors as he could in his circle. The young students were always grateful for the invitations.

As for all newcomers, there were many moments of learning. When it came time for Jane to learn to drive, Charles undertook the task of instruction himself. Having recently obtained a license after studying with a fellow medical resident, he believed himself qualified to instruct. He had just traded in his gas-guzzling Chevrolet automatic for a fuel-efficient, standard-shift Volkswagen Beetle and he'd had no problems operating either car. All progressed smoothly with the lessons, even with the complexities of learning to drive using a standard shift vehicle.

At the examination, after her test, Jane returned to the waiting room of the Driving Skills Testing Centre sans certificate.

Charles asked, "What happened?"

"Well, among other things, the examiner said that you're not supposed to be in neutral when you turn," she replied quietly.

"Oh . . ." Charles's face turned red. He had been under the impression that shifting into neutral would help save gas.

He also learned that here in the West, the sun was not red as he had been taught, and as depicted in the Japanese flag, but yellow!

Charles found his textbook English woefully inadequate in America. Understanding the accents and slang of the black patients he encountered in Chicago and Detroit was difficult. He would recall looking up "charley horse" in his dictionary of idioms after a frustrating session with a homeless man. He frequently consulted three reference books—a standard English-Japanese dictionary, an English-English dictionary, and a book of idioms. With diligent study, he gradually learned to manage almost any medical situation.

What was more difficult to master was the ease with which

the educated North Americans he encountered were able to make impromptu speeches. Accustomed to a system where written examinations and rote learning were the norm, Charles found it incredible that doctors could make speeches without preparation and he found the oral exams that were commonplace during his training nerve-wracking. Public speaking was a skill that he strove to acquire and the quest for eloquence would remain an aspiration for many years. Eventually, he would be able to speak competently and without much anxiety when the need arose.

He found the friendly interactions between senior doctors and young interns very disconcerting. It took months for him to adapt to the idea that being on a first-name basis with his superiors did not signify disrespect. Traditionally, Asian students "walked behind their teachers, not even daring to step on their shadows."

And he found the contrast between the stifling political atmosphere of Taiwan and the freedom of thought and action of 1960s America remarkably refreshing. When John F Kennedy was assassinated, Charles was amazed to find out that the president had been riding in an open car. Hatred of the ruling KMT in Taiwan by the locals ensured that Chiang Kai-Shek and his top officials did not venture out in public without heavy protection.

The anger of the African Americans against entrenched racism mirrored the frustration of the Taiwanese against the KMT government. The fact that militancy was not immediately crushed in America by the government was an eye-opening experience for young men and women who had not known anything but resentful obedience in a society where even mild opposition meant harassment, imprisonment, and sometimes death. Charles came to admire the nonviolent methods of Martin Luther King Jr all the more. Though he did not have any black friends, the indigent patients he treated in Chicago and Detroit showed Charles first-hand the plight of the underprivileged. That a man could persevere with pacifist ideals after suffering the cruel treatment of blacks in the segregated south was truly remarkable.

It was then that the seeds of activism were planted within many of these early Taiwanese immigrants. Demonstrations against the Vietnam War, the struggle for women's rights, youth protests against the "establishment," and uncensored access to books such as George Kerr's *Formosa Betrayed* and other writing regarding the KMT government galvanized some of them into action. A strong Taiwanese independence movement developed in North America as the decade wore on.

For Charles, his "awakening" had a more personal connection and was rooted not in North America but in Japan, for he had reconnected with Teacher Wang. After escaping to Japan, Wang Yude resumed his studies in Taiwanese language, eventually earning a PhD from the University of Tokyo in 1969. Concurrent with his pursuit of an academic career, Wang was also heavily involved in the Taiwanese independence movement. In 1960, he established the Taiwan Youth Association and began publishing *Taiwan Youth*, an influential journal written in Japanese with some later editions in Chinese and English. As the publication began to gain a wider circulation in Japan, Europe and North America, the dangers of being on its mailing list increased.

It was well known among the overseas Taiwanese that the KMT had a network of spies in the United States. These "professional students" kept tabs on possible troublemakers among the growing numbers of students pursuing advanced degrees abroad. There was reason to be nervous about being added to the KMT blacklist. A 1960 Taiwanese government report had listed over 120,000 people as "disappeared" since the establishment of martial law.[8] Despite the dangers, Charles remained on the mailing list of the magazine and gradually began his education in Taiwanese politics. In the ensuing years, he would become well versed in the arguments for Taiwanese independence. His views remain chiefly unchanged today.

There is a lack of clarity regarding the legal status of the island. Independence advocates maintain that at the end of the Second World War, Taiwan was not officially "returned" to China. They argue that Taiwan could not be "returned," since the defunct Qing dynasty China that gave up Formosa to Japan in 1895 was not the same nation as the Republic of China fighting the Second World War. They also point out that the 1943 Cairo Declaration, a press release issued by the United States, Great Britain, and Nationalist China regarding postwar land division, was not signed by any of the three nations and certainly not by Japan, who still held title over the island. The declaration only stated the intention of the Allies: "Japan shall be stripped of all the islands in the Pacific which she has seized or occupied since the beginning of the First World War in 1914, and that all the territories Japan has stolen from the Chinese, such as Manchuria, Formosa, and the Pescadores, shall be restored to the Republic of China."[9] Furthermore, subsequent documents such as the Yalta Declaration, Potsdam Declaration, and the 1945 Japanese Instrument of Surrender were either silent on the subject of Taiwanese sovereignty or did not explicitly transfer sovereignty to the Republic of China. Even the 1951 San Francisco Peace Treaty, in which Japan renounced all claims to Taiwan and identified the United States as the "principal occupying Power," did not specify what nation had sovereignty over the island.[10]

Independence activists also contend that the surrender of Japanese forces in Taiwan to Chiang's Nationalists was done under the direction of General MacArthur, Supreme Commander of the Allied Forces, and Chiang was merely following orders to effect Japanese capitulation, not accepting the retrocession of a part of Chinese territory. In fact, the 1945 Act of Surrender for the China

Theatre specifically authorized Chiang to accept the surrender of Japanese troops in three distinct regions: China, French Indochina, and Formosa—clearly indicating that the Allies did not consider Taiwan as a part of China at the end of the war.[11]

This view of Taiwan as separate from China was not new. After Taiwan was ceded to Japan at the end of the First Sino-Japanese War, China excluded the island from its territorial realm. By the 1930s, China saw Taiwan as an independent nation, albeit with inhabitants of Chinese descent, fighting for freedom from the fetters of Japanese colonialism. At the height of the Second Sino-Japanese War, several Chinese publications urged "weak and small nations" such as Korea, Mongolia, and Taiwan to stand together alongside China against the Japanese.[12] In 1936, Communist leader Mao Zedong did not consider Taiwan to be a "lost" Chinese territory.[13] In fact, he enthusiastically offered help in Taiwan's fight for independence from the Japanese.[14] Likewise, nationalist government documents also regarded Taiwan as a modern and foreign state outside of China's borders. Amoy mayor, Li Shilin, of Fujian province wrote in 1937 that Taiwan was traditionally seen as "a place outside the frontier" even prior to Japanese rule.[15] To the politicians of the time, Chinese were distinctly separate from Taiwanese.

It was not until 1942 that the ruling elite of the Chinese Nationalists and Communists began to regard Taiwan with more than passing interest. That year, newspapers from both parties began publishing articles supporting the recovery of Taiwan from Japan after the war. In November 1942, Nationalist foreign minister, T V Soong, announced a new Nationalist policy that stated China's expectations regarding Taiwan should the Allies win the war.[16] After the 1949 Nationalist defeat in the Chinese civil war and the formation of the People's Republic of China, Communist China continued along the same lines as their predecessor and renewed Chinese claims over Taiwan. By then, Chiang Kai-Shek had retreated to the island and formed a government-in-exile with the remnants of the Republic of China that once ruled the entire mainland. The Communists looked forward to taking over Taiwan and completing their rout of the KMT.

A referendum at that time would no doubt have resulted in the Taiwanese choosing independence.[17] But any hopes of the native Taiwanese establishing their own government were dashed as the Cold War intensified; the Americans saw Chiang's government as a necessary evil in maintaining security against the Sino-Soviet bloc in the region. For the United States, denying Communist China control of Taiwan was more important than ridding the island of the KMT.[18] Chiang was to keep Taiwan under martial law until his death in 1975 and his son took over the presidency. Martial law would not be lifted until 1987.

In the early 1960s, Charles was just beginning to understand the complexities of Taiwan's political status. Naturally, as the father of two young children, he was more focused on his medical career than political activism. His first priority was to provide for his family. That meant becoming a certified specialist as soon as he could.

Charles's guiding values in his medical practice were formed during his training in Chicago and Detroit: good communications, a caring attitude, and vigilance about details. As an obstetrician, he felt a particular obligation to adhere to these beliefs since he was responsible for two lives, not just one. With these principles he embarked upon a successful medical career.

But that career would not be on American soil. His visa ran out in 1964, and he was not prepared to go through the complicated processes of returning to Taiwan to extend it, or hiring a lawyer to seek an exemption. Instead he applied to enter Canada as an immigrant and served an additional year as a trainee in order to meet

Canadian licensing requirements. The Yangs lived for eight months in Kingston, Ontario, while Charles was a fellow at Queen's University Medical School. He then studied the temperature charts of the entire country and considered the likelihood of where he would be licensed, and chose Vancouver as a place to settle. In 1965, Charles, Jane, Mark, and Nancy moved to the milder climes of the Lower Mainland of British Columbia. Shortly after, he took the train east to Montreal and accomplished the challenging feat of passing the oral examinations to qualify both as a fellow of the Royal College of Surgeons and a licensee with the Medical Council of Canada. After a brief stint at Grace Hospital and the BC Cancer Institute, Charles began a thirty-three year career with the newly opened Richmond General Hospital in 1966. The Yangs' third child, Grace, was born in Vancouver.

In choosing private practice, Charles had to overcome the prejudices left over from his Japanese education. For his father's generation, the most respected physicians had been researchers affiliated with universities, not those who had their own practices. Japanese and German professors of medicine were held in the highest esteem. This "gown (academic) and town (private practice)" distinction was one that Charles found difficult to relinquish and he agonized over the decision. He had been asked by the chairman of the Ob-Gyn department at the University of British Columbia if he would be interested in pursuing a research career. In the end, though he was attracted to academic medicine, Charles felt that private practice would suit him better. To a man with a young family, the hours required to fulfill the imperative to "publish or perish" in academia seemed daunting. In any case, another matter began to call to him. In the decades to come, despite the many demands on him as father and doctor, Charles found himself increasingly drawn to politics. By the beginning of the 1970s, he had two passions—medicine and Taiwanese issues.

· 10 ·

A Quest for Respect

The bus stopped with a jolt and Charles's glasses, hinged on top of the smooth, white cardboard mask over his face, began to slip, so he quickly removed both and switched the order. With the mask on top of his glasses, his peripheral vision was greatly impeded but at least it was better than the glasses falling off completely. He made his way off the chartered bus with the others and was hit by a blast of chilly air. He zipped up his winter jacket and pulled on his gloves, glad the afternoon was clear. It would have been a miserable protest if typical winter rains had prevailed. The Seattle organizers and their contingent were waiting in the open-air parking lot. Placards were distributed, homemade cardboard signs mounted on foot-long wooden sticks. His sign read "Stop religious persecution in Taiwan." A woman wearing a plaid coat had one that said "Taiwan belongs to Taiwanese." Others had similar messages such as "Stop Political Repression in Taiwan" and "Free Hundreds of Dissidents and Clergymen in Taiwan." The group of about seventy-five Taiwanese

Canadians and Americans garnered curious glances from shoppers as they marched from the downtown parking lot to the corner of Third and James Streets, arriving at 607 Third Street, the Lyon Building. The red-brick structure with its terracotta frieze and cornices housed five storeys of offices above a row of shops on the street level. One of the offices belonged to the KMT Coordination Council for North American Affairs.

That the office was not an embassy was one of the humiliations that Taiwan had suffered in the past decade. In 1950, soon after the Communist victory in China, the People's Republic of China (PRC) demanded that they take the place of the Republic of China (ROC), i.e. Taiwan, at the United Nations. Both Mao's PRC and Chiang's ROC claimed to be the only legitimate government of the whole of China, a territory that included both the mainland and Taiwan.[1] As an ally of the ROC and in the midst of the Cold War, the United States sided with Chiang. With American backing, Chiang's KMT government continued to hold the Chinese seat at the United Nations as well as one of the five permanent seats on the United Nations Security Council while the PRC was denied representation. However, support for the PRC's admission among UN members began to grow in the two decades following.

Throughout the 1960s, Chiang Kai-Shek stubbornly clung to the notion that the KMT was the legitimate government of all of China and he would one day "retake the mainland." Even as the international community gradually accepted the reality of Communist China and the United States was warming up to the idea of recognizing Beijing, Chiang continued to insist on being the sole representative of China at the United Nations. He repeatedly rejected American suggestions of one UN seat for the PRC and another for Taiwan, thus squandering Taiwan's best chances for continued international representation.[2] By 1970, Beijing's support had grown to the point where more than half of United Nations General Assembly

member states recognized the PRC as the only legitimate representative of China and a vote on the matter was imminent, with China's
victory likely.[3] To avoid the indignity of being expelled, Chiang
ordered the ROC delegation to walk out of the UN ahead of a vote
in 1971, leaving the seat vacant for the PRC. It was the first of many
other losses in international recognition to come.

The most grievous setback occurred in 1978 when the United
States declared that it would be severing diplomatic ties with Taiwan
and establishing formal relations with the PRC. The United States-
Taiwan mutual defense treaty was thereby nullified. Anti-American
protests broke out in Taiwan as the shock of President Carter's
announcement unleashed fear and anger among the Taiwanese.
Though American public reaction to the Carter declaration was
mixed, bipartisan support for replacement legislation was strong and
Congress quickly drafted the Taiwan Relations Act, which permitted the continuation of weapons sales to Taiwan. The 1979 Act also
allowed unofficial diplomatic relations to be maintained between
the United States and Taiwan. The American Institute in Taiwan
was established as the agency for commercial and cultural interactions with Taipei. Likewise, the Coordination Council for North
American Affairs[4] replaced Taiwan's former consulates in several
major American cities.[5] So instead of official diplomatic offices,
North American Taiwanese were forced to conduct consular business
through the pseudo-embassies. There wasn't even one in Vancouver
or else the Canadians would have held their demonstration there.[6]
Instead they had to bus down to Seattle to make their views known.

On this Saturday in 1980, Charles and the other demonstrators milled in front of the Lyon Building, blocking the sloping
sidewalk. Several police officers guarded the entrance to the building; there had apparently been some damage to the building lobby
at another demonstration the month before. Charles watched as a
group of protesters made their way across the street to the Seattle

Public Safety Building. Photographers, reporters, and policemen began arriving. The photographer from *The Seattle Times* had already snapped a picture of the march earlier.[7]

Charles watched one of the men in front of the Public Safety Building unfurl a Nationalist flag with its red background and blue canton bearing a white sun. Another man took out a lighter and the flag went up in flames. Charles could smell the acrid smoke of the burning cloth even from across the street. The police gathered nearby but did not intervene. A third man set fire to a cardboard drawing of Chiang Ching-Kuo, and the crowd cheered. Photographers continued to snap pictures and television cameramen to film the scene.

Suddenly, a number of demonstrators ran down the street toward a car parked a short distance away. Charles and his friends ran to the corner to get a better view. The earlier group had swarmed the vehicle and were angrily banging on the sides of the car.

"What's going on?" Charles asked an onlooker.

"KMT spies taking pictures of us," the man replied.

The car peeled away from the curb and departed.

When a Seattle television station requested an interview, none of the protesters were prepared to appear without a mask. However, the station representative insisted on a spokesperson without a disguise. The Taiwanese protesters looked at each other, passing the buck, and finally someone put Charles's name forward.

Charles considered the dangers. There was the blacklist. He had probably come to the attention of the KMT as soon as he was added to the *Taiwan Youth* mailing list. Perhaps they had put him on the blacklist then or perhaps they had waited until he became a member of the Taiwanese Association, in 1966.[8] The first meeting of the Vancouver chapter was held in the Yang home under the pretext of a welcome dinner for biochemistry professor Dr Sung and his family. Charles thought if he weren't already on the blacklist, giving an American television interview would surely land him prominently on it. Many activists, upon return to Taiwan, were promptly charged with planning to overthrow the government and spreading Communist propaganda. Some were tried in military court.[9]

Others took to radical means of protest. On April 24, 1970, two members of the World United Formosans for Independence (WUFI), Peter Huang,[10] a graduate student in journalism at Cornell University, and his brother-in-law Cheng Tzu-Tsai,[11] an architect, attempted to assassinate Chiang Ching-Kuo, then head of the Taiwanese secret police and vice premier, while Chiang was on a state visit to America. During a demonstration in New York, Huang got close enough and fired a shot at Chiang. Both Cheng and Huang were arrested on the spot. Bail was granted and the North American Taiwanese raised large sums for that purpose. Charles donated one month's salary, but an acquaintance even mortgaged his house to contribute funds.

Though rash, the Chiang assassination attempt had drawn media attention to the Taiwanese democracy movement. Throughout the 1970s, support in the form of overseas independence organizations, anti-KMT publications, and monetary contributions by the Taiwanese in North America, Europe, and Japan grew.

Charles had done what he could since he arrived in North America, small though his efforts were. Even in his medical profession, inconvenient circumstances had not stopped Charles before. He had become accustomed to juggling the pressures of work with his other interests, namely protesting for better conditions in Taiwan. It was impossible for him to stand by and do nothing about the oppressive situation in the land of his birth. Now was an opportunity to do more. What was a little interview considering what others had already done? Someone had to speak and, as the reporter said, it would have more impact if the speaker would identify himself. As he stood undecided, Charles wondered what form KMT retaliation might take. He thought about his siblings and parents. They were already in Canada or the United States. The KMT would not be able to violate their rights or prevent them from leaving Taiwan. His wife and children were also safe in Canada. In North America, his loved ones were securely out of the KMT's grasp.

Charles stepped up to the reporter and took off his mask. He gave his name as CC Yang, a physician from Vancouver, BC.

The cameras rolled and Charles said, "We came to demonstrate against a totalitarian and dictatorial regime. We mourn the death of democracy in Taiwan."

He stated the aim of the protests: to alert the public to the Kaohsiung Incident and other human rights violations in Taiwan.

The Seattle Times Sunday report the following day summarized his speech thus:

> Dr CC Yang, Vancouver, decried the "torture" of political dissidents and clergymen arrested after the December 10 Human Rights Day celebration in Kaohsiung.

The Kaohsiung Incident that precipitated the Seattle demonstration had become one of the landmarks of the democracy movement.

After the KMT's disastrous defeat in the UN, the disenchanted Taiwanese middle class became increasingly assertive in the 1970s. Native Taiwanese politicians such as Huang Hsin-chieh, Kang Ning-hsiang, and Chang Chun-hung formally ran for office as Tangwai. In 1977, the populace took to the streets to protest apparent vote rigging by the KMT in Chungli Township and a riot ensued.[12] Other demonstrations led by college professors demanding political reform took place in its wake. The KMT, now under the leadership of Chang Ching-Kuo, responded by firing the professors and arresting political activists.[13]

Human rights conditions had prompted the Taiwanese

Presbyterian Church to take the unprecedented step of issu-
ing a number of declarations. Until the late 1960s, the church had
adopted the Calvinist attitude of obeying state regulations even in
the face of tyrannical rule. But with the rise of new church leaders
who subscribed to a liberal democratic theology, political activism
became part of the church's philosophy.[14] In 1971, the Presbyterian
Church of Taiwan issued a statement calling for a total revision of
the national legislature, respect for human rights, and self-determi-
nation for Taiwan. This was followed in 1975 by a demand for freedom of religion, the KMT having banned Bibles written in roman-
ized Taiwanese. A third declaration in 1977 urged independence for
Taiwan. In 1980, the secretary-general of the church, Kao Chun-
ming, was arrested and sentenced to seven years in prison.[15]

Overseas, underground networks for conveying information about
political dissidents in Taiwan were established. By the 1980s there
were over a hundred organizations and publications, mostly based in
Japan and the United States, drawing attention to Taiwan's human
rights and political conditions. Amnesty International investigated
abuses of political prisoners and monitored trials throughout the
1970s. Foreign media and politicians also began to take an interest.[16]

In 1979, a new political magazine *Meilidao* (*Beautiful Island*, also
known as *Formosa Magazine*) began publication in Taiwan. Founded
by Tangwai politicians Huang Hsin-chieh and Shi Ming-teh, the
periodical also functioned as an informal political organization.[17]
It quickly gained a wide circulation and the proceeds went toward
establishing twelve offices which served as meeting places for political discourse around the island.[18] That year, *Meilidao* planned a rally
to mark International Human Rights Day and also to protest against
the postponement of the national elections. Failing to get a permit,
the organizers went ahead with the rally. Thousands of people gathered in Kaohsiung to demonstrate and listen to speeches. Riot police
fired upon the crowd, drove vehicles into it, and blocked the exits.

At the time of the Seattle demonstration, the chief organizers of the Kaohsiung Incident were awaiting trial for sedition.[19] Based on confessions obtained through torture, the accused were sentenced to prison terms ranging from twelve years to life.[20]

As a result of his interview, Charles was put on the blacklist and would be denied visas to Taiwan for the next two decades.[21] He tried twice to return for visits and eventually gave up. When his mother vacationed in Taiwan, she was invited for several "tea chats" with the local police. Charles considered the consequences of his actions mild, and though he would later be proud to have been put on the list, for many others the blacklist brought back only painful memories.[22] Blocked entrance to their homeland was particularly agonising for activists who still had family there.

Even though the consequences for Charles turned out not life-threatening, they could have been. In the summer of 1981, Chen Wen-chen,[23] a thirty-one-year-old mathematics professor at Carnegie-Mellon University, visited Taipei with his wife and one-year-old son. A democracy activist and Taiwanese national, Chen was denied an exit permit for return to the United States and taken for questioning by the Taiwan Garrison Command[24] on July 2. His body was found on the campus of National Taiwan University the following day. The purported cause was a fall.

Another tragic case, involving Lin Yi-hsiung, took place on February 28, 1980, a month after the Seattle demonstration. An unknown assailant broke into the Lin family home in Taipei and attacked Lin's mother, seven-year-old twin daughters, and nine-year-old daughter. The only survivor of the violence was Lin's eldest daughter who later recovered from the six stab wounds that she had suffered. At the time of the attack, Lin's home had been under surveillance by the KMT while Lin was being held for his role in the Kaohsiung Incident.[25]

Another incident actually occurred in the United States, in the

San Francisco suburb of Daly City in 1984. Born in China, Henry Liu[26] was a veteran journalist who had made his way to Taiwan and then to the United States, eventually becoming an American citizen. A vocal critic of the KMT government, Liu had written an unauthorized biography of Chiang Ching-Kuo. In October 1984, Liu was shot dead in his own garage. The assassins were members of the United Bamboo Gang. Chen Chi-Li,[27] leader of the large Taipei-based gang composed mostly of Mainlanders, had been recruited by the KMT.[28]

At a 1985 congressional hearing dealing with the Liu murder, Congressman Stephen Solarz expressed his outrage that an American citizen could be killed on American soil on the orders of a foreign government.[29] He proposed legislation to bar arms sales to any governments that harassed or intimidated individuals in the United States.

As more and more countries gave official recognition to the People's Republic of China, and Taiwan became increasingly isolated, Chiang Ching-Kuo began to feel the international and domestic pressures for improvements. In 1985, the now seventy-five-year-old president declared that none of his sons would succeed him as head of state and a military regime would no longer rule Taiwan. Chiang embarked on a series of reforms which included lifting sanctions on freedoms of speech and assembly, putting restrictions on the secret police, and eventually lifting martial law in 1987. Despite opposition from conservative factions of the KMT, Chiang's hand-picked successor, a native Taiwanese Presbyterian called Lee Teng-hui, became president upon Chiang's death in 1988.[30]

Looking back, Charles was proud to have supported the independence movement in his small way. In fact, he, like many of the activists who had come through his home, was still very clear about the proper direction for Taiwan. He was no longer in contact with many of them. Still, he believed they had stayed on course. Certainly, pioneers of the independence movement were still faithful to the cause. Many still returned to Taiwan to vote during crucial elections, hoping for a government that would eventually lead Taiwan to independence.

Charles agreed with many others that the status quo, in which Taiwan existed without international recognition as a sovereign nation, was dangerous. If China were a true democracy, then the possibility of Taiwan's becoming a part of China might not be so frightening. However, given the current situation, it was crucial for Taiwan to gain a United Nations seat and end its diplomatic isolation. Polls showing that the majority of Taiwanese favoured maintaining the status quo greatly disturbed Charles and other independence advocates. He likened the increasing economic dependence of Taiwan on the Chinese market and the gradual encroachment of Chinese influence into Taiwanese life to a frog being gradually boiled in a pot of warming water. He feared that China would ultimately attain its goal of unification with Taiwan through "silent annexation."[31] and thwart the Taiwanese dream of two internationally recognized sovereign states, that of "one China" and one Taiwan.

When the Canadian government deemed Taiwan a "pariah state" alongside North Korea,[32] when American judges categorized Taiwanese nationals as being in "political purgatory" or as "stateless persons,"[33] and when Taiwanese athletes suffered the humiliation of competing internationally under the misnomer of Chinese Taipei instead of Taiwan, Charles was clear about the path that Taiwan needed to take. Surely the Taiwanese deserved the respect accorded to nations with much smaller populations. Taiwan's population was larger than three quarters of all UN member states.[34]

What was the alternative? Was Taiwan to give up its democratic and just society, as it now was, to return to a nation that had changed beyond recognition from the 1895 China when the island was still within its dominion? Who would want to give up Taiwan's hard-won democracy to regress to a government where human rights were still routinely disregarded? To belong to a nation where Falun Gong adherents were persecuted, where black jails existed, where accounts of the Tiananmen Massacre had been purposely erased from public memory, where internet users routinely had to skirt restrictions on freedom of expression, where Tibetans and Uyghurs were treated harshly, and where the Chinese Communist Party still ruled supreme in a newly capitalist society. No matter what promises China made to bring Taiwan under its control, was it to be trusted? Witness China's reluctance to honour its "one country, two systems" agreement with Hong Kong. A government that had never ruled Taiwan even for a day was claiming the island as its own on the basis of national boundaries that had not been in effect since 1895. It frustrated Charles that, given China's long history of shifting national borders, the Communist government would not respect Taiwan's status as an independent nation.

When Charles recalled the days when democracy seemed out of reach, Taiwan's progress from martial law to today's young democracy amazed him. Granted, there were still problems with Taiwanese democracy: vote buying, nepotism, corruption, and so on. The KMT remained the world's wealthiest political party and continued to wield power regardless of whether they were in government. It would take time for Taiwan's political system to mature. It used to embarrass Charles to see overseas reports of brawls breaking out in the Taiwanese legislature. But then Peng Ming-min has pointed out that, in the British House of Commons, the distance across the floor between the government and opposition benches was two sword lengths apart, a holdover from the days when parliamentarians routinely carried weapons and disagreements sometimes escalated to violence.[35] It heartened Charles when he saw students in the Sunflower movement conduct their protests peacefully and effectively.[36] He placed his hopes in the next generations.

A Taiwanese Canadian

RICHMOND, BRITISH COLUMBIA – JUNE 24, 2015

After breakfast, Charles sat on the couch in his living room surrounded by newspapers and with his iPad to begin the most enjoyable part of his day. He opened the *Vancouver Sun* and browsed through the headlines, stopping at the editorial advocating tax reforms, entitled, "Tax fairness needs to be a priority for Ottawa." The writer wanted to ensure that wealthy Chinese immigrants were paying their proper share of taxes. The example the author had chosen was close to home. According to Statistics Canada, in the Thompson area of Richmond, where there was a high proportion of recent Chinese immigrants living in houses valued at over a million dollars, over a quarter of the residents, many of them owners of these houses, reported incomes close to the poverty level.[1] Charles felt a familiar mixture of indignation and frustration sweep over him.

This was not the first time he had felt helpless against the actions of the Mainlander Chinese. He wished to see the Chinese as more honest, more altruistic, less corrupt. Given his experiences in Taiwan, it was hard for him to set aside his prejudices against Mainlanders. The native Taiwanese who had lived under Japanese rule had bemoaned the loss of "clean government" when Mainlanders took over the island. The corrupt practices endemic in the Kuomintang party throughout its presence in mainland China soon became prevalent within the Taiwanese bureaucracy after the Second World War. Vote-buying, influence-peddling, bribery, and other ills still plagued Taiwan, especially because the KMT was the richest political party in the world, due largely to the assets they had confiscated from the Japanese upon assumption of power. In today's China, the problem was even worse than in Taiwan. It was hard to go a day without hearing reports of another corrupt official being exposed or reading stories of citizens who had gotten rich through illegal means. Charles wanted to distinguish himself from these Chinese, to say he was different. That he was as outraged about the abuses of the recent immigrants as any other Canadian.

Still, he could not allocate the blame solely to Mainlanders. There were groups of Taiwanese who also took advantage of the Canadian system. He recalled a conversation he'd had with a Taiwanese immigrant over a decade ago. He had been invited for dinner at the townhouse of one of the men in his Taiwanese seniors' group. Mr X had come to Canada in the 1990s after his retirement from some unknown occupation in Taiwan. His children had sponsored his wife and him under the Family Reunification program, but they did not need to provide for their elderly parents. Instead, the couple lived in a government-subsidized rental building and were collecting social benefits meant for seniors living below the poverty line. After meeting the ten-year residency requirement, the two now also collected Old Age Security Pension courtesy of Canadian taxpayers. They got around town using discounted bus passes available only to "low income" seniors. And yet, they owned a Mercedes and Charles was certain they had significant assets in Taiwan.

"The money is there for the taking. You're foolish if you don't," Mr X said.

It seemed that deception was a common practice among new immigrants. According to Hong Kong's *South China Morning Post*, Canada's now defunct Immigrant Investor Programme had allowed almost 30,000 immigrants with substantial assets to enter British Columbia since 2005.[2] Of these, roughly half, most of them Mainlanders, had entered BC illegally by applying to settle in Quebec or elsewhere instead of their true destination. It had cost British Columbians billions of dollars in their share of the loans provided to the federal government by the investor immigrants.

Recently, the *Vancouver Sun* had been dominated by stories about rising real estate prices in Greater Vancouver,[3] allegedly driven by foreign buyers with ready cash edging out local bidders, especially for detached single-family homes. The mayor of Vancouver had called for an anti-speculation tax to prevent "flipping" of real estate in the city and now there was talk of imposing taxes on absentee titlehold-ers and higher property transfer levies for foreign owners.[4]

It reminded Charles of the "monster house" debate in the 1980s and 90s. Back then, well-to-do businessmen from Taiwan and Hong Kong, not mainland Chinese, had made up the majority of buyers. Developers, responding to demand from the market, began buying up property in established neighourhoods, including the exclusive area of Shaughnessy, tearing down the English-style homes and replacing them with larger houses. These new homes often featured wok kitchens, four to six bedrooms, spiral staircases, and were built in accordance with the principles of *feng shui*. Sometimes old trees were cut down to accommodate the expanded foundations of the new homes. The locals responded by launching multiple complaints with Vancouver city council regarding the incompatibility of the new houses with the existing character of their neighbourhoods and call-ing for bylaws to regulate the size of allowable housing. The builders retorted by declaring the downzoning proposals discriminatory and racist.[5]

Given BC's racist history, these charges further inflamed the situation. After all, Canada was the country that had enacted legislation like the 1923 Chinese Immigration Act, sometimes known as the Chinese Exclusion Act, at the behest of racists in British Columbia. As a result, Chinese immigration to Canada virtually stopped during the interwar years. Though the Act lifted the hated head tax on Chinese immigrants that had been in place since 1885 (also instituted under pressure from BC), it narrowly restricted entry to a small group of Chinese such as diplomats, specific students, and specialized merchants. An estimated 15 Chinese immigrants were allowed into Canada between 1923 and 1947, when the Act was finally repealed (partly to recognize the contributions that Chinese Canadian soldiers had made to the Second World War and also because China had been allied with the United States and Canada during the war).[6]

But the people resisting the rapid changes in Richmond were not necessarily racists. Charles sympathized with his white neighbour who said he felt like a stranger in his own hometown. It was the shock of the pace of change that was prompting the backlash. Even Charles, accustomed to rapid shifts in circumstances, felt the radical alterations were too quick. And yet, global forces were resulting in changes that seemed uncontrollable by local governments.

In 1962, the Canadian government introduced the first immigration regulations that removed outright racism. Applicants were judged on the basis of skills instead of countries of origin. The points system introduced in 1967 formalized a more objective evaluation process for immigrant admission where education, occupation, age, English or French language proficiency, character, and employment prospects were assessed.[7] The 1976 Immigration Act allowed independents to apply as refugees and for family reunification and was again based on principles of racial tolerance.[8] The number of

Taiwanese immigrants arriving peaked in the late 1980s and 1990s after the Canadian government introduced the Immigrant Investor Program in 1985. A 2001 survey showed that eighty percent of the Taiwanese then living in Canada had arrived during the 1990s.[9] Along with students and skilled workers, there were a large number of wealthy business owners who immigrated during this time. Some have settled, some have returned to Taiwan, and some continue to travel between their two homes.

The sheer number of Chinese faces on the streets of Richmond never failed to astonish Charles afresh. He recalled the 1960s when the number of Taiwanese in Vancouver numbered just about a hundred and his friends in the community were mostly families of professors and students. These pioneers had made their homes here and had no plans to return to Taiwan. That historical experience became the stuff of books and film. Dong Fangbai's (東方白) three-volume novel, *Sand in the Waves* (浪淘沙), told the story of a woman born in northern Taiwan during the Japanese colonial period.[10] Coming from a well-to-do family supportive of her education, Cai was given the unusual privilege of attending school, first in the Japanese elementary school system then in a Presbyterian mission school staffed by Canadians. There she acquired English to augment her Taiwanese and Japanese language skills. She continued her education in Japan and, after obtaining her degree from Tokyo Women's Medical School, returned to Taiwan to practice as an obstetrician. She spent a short time in China before enrolling in the University of Toronto's School of Hygiene in 1941. As war loomed, Cai quit her studies and travelled to Vancouver, hoping to find a passage back to Taiwan. When the Pacific war broke out, she was forced to stay in Canada for five years because the passenger ship service to Asia was discontinued. As a Japanese citizen, she was classified as an enemy and could only find steady work as a physician in the Slocan Japanese internment camp of British Columbia during the war years. When she finally made her way back to Taiwan, she found KMT persecution insufferable and, after a marriage of convenience to Canadian Presbyterian minister Reverend George Gibson, returned to Vancouver in 1953, where she would live until her death in 1990. The novel was made into a Taiwanese television series in 2005.

Most of the Taiwanese pioneers of Vancouver did not lead such eventful lives. As a group, they were upstanding citizens: doctors, engineers, academics, and ordinary working folk—part of the model minority. With the huge influx of Taiwanese in the 1990s, there was a need to help new immigrants adapt to Canadian life. Charles, along with core members of the Taiwanese Canadian Association, helped co-found the Taiwanese Canadian Cultural Society (TCCS) in 1991, a nonprofit organization devoted to immigrant assistance and the promotion of Taiwanese culture in Canada. Charles had served on the board of TCCS for close to a decade. This society and the Taiwanese Canadian Association were close to his heart.

The controversies surrounding the real-estate acquisitions by the Chinese made Charles examine his loyalties and, despite his experiences elsewhere, he reacted as a "homegrown" Canadian. He resented the rapid changes. He decried the increasing unaffordability of Greater Vancouver for young people. And he particularly resented those who only "took" from Canada. He had tried to contribute to his adopted country. He had made a point of attending the mainstream Richmond Presbyterian Church and served as an elder for four decades, seven years of which as a representative to the Presbytery of Westminster. He had been on Special Commissions for the Presbytery dealing with issues within the Vancouver Taiwanese Presbyterian Church, inevitably acting as a liaison because of his language abilities. He had been appointed to the BC Advisory Council on Multiculturalism in 2000 and reported to the minister for three years. He had written many letters to newspapers to educate other Canadians about Taiwanese culture and to advocate for Taiwan's place in the world.

Charles felt strongly that immigration should not be for the sole purpose of possessing a second passport so as to ensure a safe retreat in the event of trouble at home. He preferred to translate the Japanese word for immigrants, 移住者, as "transferred living" to connote permanent residence in one's destination country. Real immigrants do not act like guests in Canada, they give back to Canadian society. The only way to earn respect from the larger Canadian society was to contribute and be a part of it. Perhaps due to his profession and his fluency in English, he had always felt welcomed and respected. He felt at home in gatherings where there were few Asians. At the same time, he was constantly aware that he was part of a visible minority. Though he had experienced little racism in a country where one-fifth of the population was part of a visible minority,[11] he could never forget he was not white.

When he lived in Manchuria and Taiwan, he was tagged as an Asian, indistinguishable from other Asians. Yet, he was an invisible minority—never feeling fully Japanese or Taiwanese. He sympathized with the Taiwanese protagonist of *Orphan of Asia* who never seemed to fit in anywhere no matter how hard he tried to be Japanese or Chinese. In Canada, Charles had been accepted as a real Taiwanese and his Taiwanese identity had crystallized. However, as a Taiwanese, he was still a minority in the greater Chinese population, lumped together with the Chinese and overwhelmed by their numbers— a minority within a minority. He wished he could fully embrace being a Canadian of Chinese descent without having to constantly distinguish himself as Taiwanese, as different from the Chinese. But because of Taiwan's uncertain political status, the Taiwanese in both Canada and the United States were forced to continue the distinction with small acts like marking Taiwanese instead of Chinese on census forms. He wished things were simpler.

But, in a country that hosted immigrants from around the world, simplicity was not the norm. Past histories and loyalties migrated with new settlers. Certainly there were internal differentiations among the Chinese. During the Second World War, many long-time Cantonese-speaking Chinatown residents across North America who had supported Sun Yat-Sen's 1911 establishment of the Republic of China were dismayed by the Communist Chinese victory. Prior to Canada's official recognition of China in 1970,[12] most Chinese Canadians had supported the KMT.[13] After both the United States and Canada replaced Taiwan with China in official diplomatic affairs, pro-China support began to grow in Chinatowns across the continent, especially as second-generation locally-born Chinese began to oppose "old world" politics in favour of mainstream political positions. In 2004, San Francisco's Chinatown played out the split between pro-China and pro-KMT factions among long-established Chinese organizations, each demonstrating their allegiances by flying either the "golden stars on red" flag of the People's Republic of China or the "white sun on blue" of the KMT, now the flag of Taiwan.[14] These age-old animosities still kept the two groups distinct and apart. Fresh division and segregation had also been introduced into Greater Vancouver with the new influx of Hong Kong and mainland Chinese and their accompanying prejudices against each other.

Even among the Taiwanese, complicated relations existed. The subgroups in Taiwan were divisible by language: the majority who spoke Hokkien (commonly referred to as Taiwanese), the smaller Hakka-speaking group, the many aboriginal tribes, and the Mandarin-speaking Mainlanders. The Taiwanese organizations that Charles belonged to, such as the Taiwanese Canadian Association and TCCS, were dominated by Hokkien speakers. When TCCS changed its bylaws to allow the admission of Mainlanders into the organization, there was considerable opposition from those who had suffered during the White Terror.

Charles was glad he had chosen Canada as his final destination. When he read of the deaths of Ferguson's Michael Brown or of New York's Eric Garner, he was again reminded of the profound racial divide in the United States. It was a deep wound that did not ever seem to heal despite the presence of a black president in the White House. The population of blacks in Vancouver was comparatively small, so overt racist acts against African Canadians did not seem to make the local news. But for the most part, Canada seemed to be able to accommodate differences peacefully. Comparing the lives of his brother in Japan and his two siblings in America with his own in Canada, Charles felt that Canada was the most livable place. Here, he did not feel the same pressures to conform as in the homogenous society of Japan and the "melting pot" of America. Here, he had earned respect as a Taiwanese Canadian and did not have to hide any part of his identity. Canada's largely successful multiculturalism policy made it stand out among nations.

His three children had adapted well in Canada. He now wondered what future generations of Yangs would look like, what their attitudes would be. They were part of the incredible Chinese diaspora that had spread out over the last century.[15] There were now more Chinese living outside of China than the entire population of France. Many of the Chinese had migrated from their first stops to Vancouver. There were ethnic Chinese from Malaysia, Singapore, the Philippines, southern Africa, Latin America (especially Peru), and the Caribbean.[16] It seemed that wherever they landed, the Chinese would adapt and evolve according to their surroundings and through intermarriage with the locals. In Chinatowns around the world, some old Chinese traditions would be retained, others lost, and new habits of thought acquired.

Ultimately, Charles's sense of belonging was derived from the Vancouver Taiwanese-Canadian community. He was firmly rooted here. His children and grandchildren were thoroughly westernized though they tried to preserve some parts of their Taiwanese identity through cultural activities. Future generations of Yangs would be Canadians. By then, maybe more of the world would be in a state where national borders did not define identity, where race and countries were irrelevant, and "foreigner" was an idea of the past. But for now, he was a proud first generation Taiwanese Canadian.

End of Life

RICHMOND, BC – NOVEMBER 2016

Sitting on the edge of his favourite armchair in his study, hemmed in by piles of books, Charles ran his hand over the red leather volume at the top of the nearest stack. Since his cataract surgery, his myopia had disappeared and he now needed only reading glasses, but the gold lettering on the gilt-trimmed book was large enough for him to read without aid: *Collected Stories of O Henry*. He picked up the book and flipped past the marbled end paper to the title page:

> *To Jane*
> *Inspired by the story "The Gifts of the Magi" so many years ago.*
> *Charles*
> *Dec 25, 94.*

Charles blinked back tears. Since his stroke, he had become emotionally labile, laughing uproariously at the most trivial incidents and crying at the most innocuous triggers. He had forgotten about this book. He recalled the first time he had read the story, in a German-language course at National Taiwan University. It seemed strange to him now that they would have chosen an American story for a course in German. It was a compulsory course in the pre-med curriculum. But he had studied German for only one year and few words of the language remained now.

Well, learning German was no stranger than Jane's reading Jane Austen at university. In translation, of course. He had already set aside the Avenel edition of Jane Austen's complete novels to give away. At one time, he had collected books, when he thought he would read them. But he rarely read fiction now, except for that chosen by the TCCS book club. In this "end of life" stage, he spent much of his time sifting through Jane's many notes and diaries. The hours of reading through her records of shared incidents, occasionally surprised by those he had never known or had forgotten, brought her closer to him.

Cliché or not, she had been his best friend, his confidante, his soul mate. For him, Jane's name (meaning: gift of God) encapsulated all. It seemed as if she'd had a direct telephone line to God. She had given him peace and comfort. They were married for fifty-three years. Her death distressed him more than all his physical ailments combined. Even now, six years after her passing, the pain remained.

He settled back in the armchair and scanned the table of contents for "Gifts of the Magi," but was confounded by the extensive list stretching across five pages. The man had been prolific! Then he noticed the yellow Post-it near the back of the book. He turned to the marked page and read the story for the first time in many years. When he reached the last paragraph, tears filled his eyes. Just like the couple in the story, Jane had given everything she could to him, "sacrificed [her] greatest treasures." In her simple way, she had given the wisest gift of all.

He had been allowed the freedom to pursue his work because she had taken care of everything else in their lives. He was grateful to her not only for raising their three children but also for ministering to his parents. It had not been easy for her. Juggling the Taiwanese expectations of his parents and the Canadian aspirations of the children had caused friction at times but she had persevered, and led by example. He was convinced that Jane had been the greatest blessing bestowed upon him by God. She had transformed him into a better man. She had shown him what true love was.

He still struggled with the guilt of not noticing her illness earlier. He was a physician, after all. If anyone should have known, it should have been him. Though his intellectual self knew that the outcome would not have been different, his emotional self still flagellated itself regularly. He should have noticed the symptoms before the loss of appetite and rapid weight-loss. She had been diagnosed with pancreatic cancer close to Christmas 2009 and passed away in April of the following year. Four short months.

Her death had occurred under the compassionate gaze of God. Her hospital visits had been as an outpatient. She had not suffered any side effects from the "palliative" chemotherapy. She had died in her own bed. All three children had been at her side when she passed. If he could choose how he would die, he would choose a death like hers. It was a mercy that the disease had progressed so quickly and she had not had to undergo futile rounds of chemotherapy with its horrendous side effects.

More importantly, she had been spared the advanced stages of Alzheimer's. Jane had begun showing early signs a few years before the cancer diagnosis. Charles had noticed the notes she'd posted next to all the telephones to remind herself that the Canadian emergency number was 911 instead of the Taiwanese 119. She had been aware of her problem. It would have been difficult to watch her decline and, even worse, to calm the accompanying frustration during times of lucidity.

Despite this knowledge, Charles felt he would never get over her death. There was a hymn called "God Be with You Till We Meet Again" to which he wholeheartedly subscribed. He believed that Jane was watching from above and he would see her soon. She would not like to see him in tears all the time. She would like to see him coping. That's why he took antidepressants to ward off the chronic pain.

Charles had spoken with a funeral director about his great sense of loss not long after Jane's death. The man had said, "You can never get over it, you can only compromise." That was true. Out of all the reading he had done on grief, the bulk of which was written by medical specialists, the most useful had been a book edited by George Bowering and Jean Baird called *The Heart Does Break: Canadian Writers on Grief and Mourning.* In Bowering's essay "May I Bring You Some Tea?" he pointed out that mourning is an expression of love for the deceased. Charles's heart had broken when Jane died. And he did not want to get over it. There was a Taiwanese phrase, *um gum,*[1] that expressed how he felt. Somehow the Taiwanese expression seemed more poignant and held more meaning than any English phrase.

He felt that she had died too young, though Jane had made preparations years in advance for their deaths as well as those of his parents. Because so many Taiwanese refuse to speak about death and funeral arrangements in the superstitious belief that death would be hastened if one spoke of it, Charles had been nervous when he approached his parents about purchasing burial plots. He had invited them to visit Ocean View Cemetery in Burnaby on the pretext that they were going to purchase plots for Jane and him. His plan was to casually suggest buying four adjoining plots. To his surprise, his parents accepted the proposal with equanimity. His mother had even joked while they were on a tour of the grounds. When the sector of predominantly Chinese plots was pointed out to them, she had rejected the idea of being buried among the mostly Cantonese immigrants. She felt, based on her bus visits to Chinatown with fellow passengers speaking loud Cantonese, that the Chinese section would be too noisy! He had been taken unawares by his mother's tongue-in-cheek humour and revelled in the unexpected levity.

Three of the plots were filled now. Soon it would be his turn.

Charles set the O Henry book down beside him, undecided about what to do with it. Should he give it away or keep it as a reminder of Jane? He looked at his watch and stirred himself. The decision would have to wait. Julia would soon be here for their interview.

When they began meeting for the biography in January 2014, he had been uncertain about the result. In all their conversations, he had been as honest as he could be and repeatedly stressed his guiding principle of humility. She said she understood and would write in as balanced a way as she could. She seemed to be taking a long time with it, though. Charles hoped he would live to see the book in print.

Where were his hearing aids? He wanted to make sure he didn't forget again. A few times before, he had done the interviews without them and misheard the questions. When he was at home, he often went without them because he would forget to take them out when he washed his face or took a shower. The hearing aids could be a nuisance but they were a necessity. At first, he had been slow to get them, not due to vanity but because of cost. Even though he'd had a successful medical practice, his lifelong habit of frugality, inculcated from childhood, had made him hesitate. His current set, purchased at a discount warehouse, retailed at double the price elsewhere.

Jane had had the same thriftiness. Up until her death, she continued to wipe plates clean with scraps of bread before dishwashing, simply because she could not bear to waste. The books and papers he was sorting through were the results of years of accumulation. Conservation that verged on hoarding. But this trait was typical of all the Taiwanese who had lived through the war. Economy was in their marrows. His shared background with Jane had made their marriage work so well. There had been so many things that needed no words.

"Ronda, can you bring me my hearing aids, please?" he called toward the kitchen.

In a few moments, the Filipino woman appeared at the doorway, hearing aids in hand.

Soon after his stroke and the onset of Jane's dementia, the children had convinced them to hire a live-in caregiver. Charles was grateful for their foresight. Ronda had been with him for almost seven years now. He was fortunate to have her; she was competent, caring, and cheerful.

"And please make sure you bring in tea and fruit sometime during the interview."

Ronda smiled and nodded before returning to the kitchen.

Someday, she would have to do more for him. At the age of eighty-four, he was still capable of personal care. Although he did everything slowly, he could still dress, use the toilet and the shower. He was doing well for someone who had survived two cancers (bladder and prostate), and a stroke, and was suffering from PLS.

The stroke had struck in September 2006. The day had begun with a visit to his parents' burial sites at Ocean View. Though he had felt dizzy then, the spell had passed. Later on, his speech became slurred, but that too passed. After chairing a meeting at the Taiwanese Cultural Centre, he visited his general practitioner, but because he seemed normal, only a CT scan was arranged. However, the next day, after he lost movement in his left leg, Charles was rushed to Emergency. He then began six months of apparent recovery—progressing from communicating with an alphabet board and drinking fluids only—to near-normal speech and diet. His mobility improved to the point where he was able to walk with a cane.

Then, to the puzzlement of his neurologists, his right leg slowly weakened. It took nearly two years and four neurologists to arrive at a diagnosis of Primary Lateral Sclerosis (PLS). Despite the competence of his doctors and because of the similarity of the two diseases, the juxtaposition of the stroke with the onset of PLS delayed the eventual diagnosis. Now his PLS was slowly progressing, and it could potentially end up as full-blown ALS, or Lou Gehrig's disease; Charles believed that he might not live to the day when that happened. Were it to occur, he could look forward to the gradual loss of neural functions: legs, hands, fingers . . . not able to speak, not able to swallow, and eventually not able to breathe without a respirator. What kind of a life would that be?

No, he was not waiting for the full onset of the disease. Like Sue Rodriguez, Gloria Taylor, and other ALS sufferers who faced miserable declines, he supported physician-assisted deaths over the alternative.[2] Despite his Christian beliefs, there was a point at which human dignity and quality of life trumped all other considerations. God would understand the meaning of mercy.

Though he likely would not opt for assisted dying, Charles would not put his children in a position where they had to consider artificial means to prolong his life, with the associated emotional and financial costs. He had gathered all three children and informed them simultaneously so there would be no ambiguity.

He had been fortunate in his offspring. His children were caring, decent people. They were solicitous and forward-looking. He would be well cared for until the end. In 2014, they had renovated his house so he could be warmer and the rooms were more wheelchair-accessible.

Charles pushed himself off the armchair and reached for his walker. He shuffled to his desk and retrieved the notebook in which he kept track of tasks for the interviews. Settling back in his chair, he flipped open the notebook. Julia had asked him to think about two questions last time: What was his legacy? What advice did he have for the next generation? A tall order.

What could one really say about one's life? He had tried to be a dutiful son, devoted father, loving husband, and diligent doctor. He was a simple man, a country boy from Taiwan. His strong sense of humility prohibited him from calling his thoughts wisdom. He had been privileged to serve, not only as a doctor but also as a Taiwanese. In that, he had done his best. It had been a pleasure. This book would be his last contribution. Loss of privacy was a small price to pay if more people could understand the plight of the Taiwanese.

Even now, he was still evolving. He delighted in ideas, in learning. These were the joys left to him. News of the Sunflower movement in Taiwan had given him hope for the country's future. His fears of China's silent annexation of Taiwan were slightly quelled by this ardent display of patriotism by a new generation of activists. His generation's dream for an independent Taiwan had not come to pass. The rise of China had hindered Taiwan's bid for international recognition as an independent state. Unreasonable Chinese actions, old and new, still irked him: when the Chinese government tried to assert sovereignty over the island and delayed international aid to Taiwan following the earthquake in 1999,[3] when the Chinese media called Chinese American ambassador Gary Locke a "rotten banana" in 2014,[4] when Taiwanese nationals who had never set foot in China were deported from Kenya to China at the insistence of Chinese authorities in August.[5] That the Chinese Communist Party had never governed Taiwan for even one day but was claiming the island as a renegade province, a sacred inalienable territory of China, and was consistently forcing Taiwan off the international stage frustrated him. Why would any nation give up democracy in favour of one-party autocratic rule? But even with the election of a DPP president in Taiwan, the chances of independence were low. Now, with the unpredictable President Trump in office in the United States, Taiwan's future seemed even more uncertain. Though the dream of Taiwanese independence was not achievable in his lifetime, Charles was glad to have witnessed the dawn of democracy in Taiwan during his sojourn in this world. The change from what he had experienced when he first reached the island in 1946 and the Taiwan of today was nothing short of miraculous.

Still, there was work to be done. He was glad to see that the struggle would continue. This new generation of Taiwanese activists had been born after the lifting of martial law in 1987. For the most part, they had enjoyed unfettered access to information, about the past and the present. Unlike him, they would not need to leave Taiwan in order to learn the truth about their own country, in order to find their identities.

That he ended up living in Vancouver, one of the most desirable cities in the world, Charles attributed not to his own prescience or wisdom but to God's plan for him. He had lived through tumultuous times unscathed; he had not lost a single member of his family during the wars or the White Terror.[6] He had been accepted in a country that allowed him multiple identities. A country that gave him the confidence that he had sought all his life, a society that helped him escape the feeling of inferiority bred under the Japanese. It was here that he had found a sense of belonging.

And it was here where he would remain. The Chinese say that a man's true home is where he wants to be buried. Charles's home was in Canada. His three children and five grandchildren were full Canadians. Some of his grandchildren were biracial while others were wholly ethnic Taiwanese. Regardless of genetic make-up, all of them spoke English better than Taiwanese and acted more Western than Asian. But for Charles, losing their Taiwanese language and culture was less important than losing their Christian values. The loss of Taiwanese heritage was inevitable; the loss of Christianity was not.

What did he have to pass on to future generations? What would they think of him? In the final analysis, he just wanted to be remembered as a fair man, personally and professionally. And he only wanted fairness for the land of his birth.

Charles closed the notebook and glanced at his watch. Julia would arrive in ten minutes. He always liked to be seated on the couch in the sitting room beforehand so they could begin on time. He pulled the walker closer and slipped the notebook into the pouch attached to its side. He struggled out of his chair and, slouching over his walker, made his way toward the stairs where he used to run up two steps at a time but but rarely ventured now. Before he had taken ten steps, he turned back toward the study. Stopping beside the chair, Charles picked up the O Henry volume and dropped it into the pouch. He'd had full use of the book; it was time to pass it on.

The Yang family, 1938. Akihisa (later Charles) in the middle.

Akihisa Takayama, 1938.

Jane in school uniform, 1938.

Jane (left) with sister in Japanese dress, 1943.

Jane with oldest child, Mark, in Taipei, 1958.

Akihisa with his schoolmates on top of 203-Metre Hill, Port Arthur (Manchuria), 1943.

National Taiwan University School of Arts building, 1950s.

The Yang ancestral home in Yongkang (Photo taken by Julia Lin 2014).

The Yang family, 1954. Front: Henry (L), Dr Yang (Charles's father), Mrs Yang, Rita. Back: Charles Yang, Masayoshi.

The Yangs' wedding, February 12, 1957, Presbyterian church (大灣基督長老教會), Yongkang (永康鄉, 大灣), Tainan.

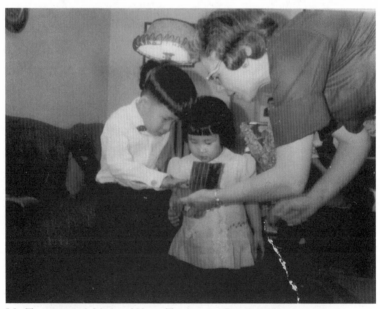

Mrs Thompson with Mark and Nancy. Thanksgiving, Detroit, 1962.

At TCCS gathering (date unknown, likely during the 2000s). From left to right, 林瑞麟, Ruey Lin, also known as Ruey Satake; founder of the Taiwanese-Canadian Historical Society, Charles Yang, and Peng Ming-min, Taiwanese independence activist.

Charles at TCCS gathering, with British Columbian politicians and Taiwanese officials, 2001.

The Yang family on a cruise, December, 2004. From left: Sean (Nancy Yang's son), Jennifer (Nancy's second daughter), Hans (Nancy's husband), Nancy Yang (Charles Yang's eldest daughter), Grace Yang (Charles Yang's second daughter), Jane, Charles, Rita (Charles' sister), Yumin (Mark's wife), Mark Yang (Charles's son), Carmen (Nancy's eldest daughter). Front: Andrew (Mark's son), Rachel (Mark's daughter).

Works Cited

Anderson, Megan. "Taiwan." *Taiwan*. University of Arizona Geosciences, 3 May 2001. Web. 25 Jan. 2015. <http://www.geo.arizona.edu/~anderson/taiwan/tai_index.html>.

Andrade, Tonio. *How Taiwan Became Chinese: Dutch, Spanish, and Han Colonization in the Seventeenth Century*. New York: Columbia UP, 2008. Print.

Barkan, Elliott Robert. *Immigrants in American History Arrival, Adaptation, and Integration*. Santa Barbara, Calif.: ABC-CLIO, 2013. Print.

Bedford, Olwen, and Guangguo Huang. *Taiwanese Identity and Democracy the Social Psychology of Taiwan's 2004 Elections*. New York, N.Y.: Palgrave Macmillan, 2006. Print.

Bessel, Richard. *Nazism and War*. New York: Modern Library, 2004. Print.

Birnbaum, Phyllis, and Ryotaro Shiba. *Clouds above the Hill A Historical Novel of the Russo-Japanese War, Volume 1*. Hoboken: Taylor and Francis, 2013. Print.

Burgos, Jonathan, and Netty Ismail. "Forget Gold, Buy a Vancouver Condo If You Want to Stash Your Wealth, Says World's Top Money Manager." *Financial Post (from Bloomberg News)*. 21 Apr. 2015. Web. 20 July 2015. <http://business.financialpost.com/personal-finance/mortgages-real-estate/forget-gold-buy-a-vancouver-condo-if-you-want-to-hoard-your-wealth-says-worlds-biggest-money-manager>.

"Cairo Conference Press Release." *Cairo Conference*. Taiwan Documents Project, 1 Dec. 1943. Web. 11 May 2015. <http://www.taiwandocuments.org/cairo.htm#par3>.

Canadian Press. "Canada's Foreign-born Population Soars to 6.8 Million." *CBCnews*. CBC/Radio Canada, 8 May 2013. Web. 21 July 2015. <http://www.cbc.ca/news/canada/canada-s-foreign-born-population-soars-to-6-8-million-1.1308179>.

Canadian Press. "Canada Day 2014: What Pariah States Made Ottawa's 'do Not Invite' List." *CBCnews*. CBC/Radio Canada, 30 June 2014. Web. 1 June 2015. <http://www.cbc.ca/news/canada/canada-day-2014-what-pariah-states-made-ottawa-s-do-not-invite-list-1.2691588>.

Chan, Yeeshan. *Abandoned Japanese in Postwar Manchuria: The Lives of War Orphans and Wives in Two Countries*. London: Routledge, 2011. Print.

Chang, Iris. *The Chinese in America: A Narrative History*. New York: Viking, 2003. Print.

Chi, Charlie. "The Surrender of Japanese Forces in the China Theatre." Taiwan Documents Project, 2002. Web. 11 May 2015. <http://www.taiwandocuments.org/japansurrender.htm>.

Chou, Wan-yao. "The 'kominka' Movement: Taiwan under Wartime Japan, 1937-1945." *ProQuest Dissertations and Theses* (Order No. 9218772, Yale University) (1991): 1-280. Print.

Chou, Wanyao, Carole Plackitt, and Tim Casey. *A New Illustrated History of Taiwan*. Taipei, Taiwan: SMC, 2015. Print.

Clulow, Adam. *Statecraft and Spectacle in East Asia: Studies in Taiwan-Japan Relations*. London: Routledge, 2011. Print.

CNA. "Status Quo Is That of Sovereign ROC: DPP Member." *Www.ChinaPost.com.tw*. The China Post, 13 Apr. 2015. Web. 1 June 2015. <http://www.chinapost.com.tw/taiwan/china-taiwan-relations/2015/04/13/433516/Status-quo.htm>.

Cull, Nicholas John, David Holbrook Culbert, and David Welch. "World War II (Japan)." *Propaganda and Mass Persuasion: A Historical Encyclopedia, 1500 to the Present*. Santa Barbara, Calif.: ABC-CLIO, 2003. 444-445. Print.

Culpan, Tim, and Adela Lin. "Taiwan Students Occupy Legislature Over China Pact." *Bloomberg.com*. Bloomberg, 19 Mar. 2014. Web. 1 June 2015. <http://www.bloomberg.com/news/articles/2014-03-19/taiwan-students-occupy-legislature-over-china-trade-pact-vote>.

Culver, Annika A. "Chapter 1: Laying the Groundwork for the Japanese Avant-garde Propogandist." *Glorify the Empire*. Vancouver BC: UBC, 2013. 11-33. Print.

Davidson, James Wheeler. *The Island of Formosa, past and Present History, People, Resources, and Commercial Prospects. Tea, Camphor, Sugar, Gold, Coal, Sulphur,*

Economical Plants, and Other Productions. London and New York: Macmillan &;, 1903. Print.

Dillon, Michael. *China a Modern History*. London: I.B. Tauris;, 2010. Print.

Dong, Fangbai. 浪淘沙. 前衛出版社, 1990. Print.

Dreyer, Edward L. *China at War, 1901-1949*. London: Longman, 1995. Print.

Editor, Vancouver Sun. "Editorial: Tax Fairness Needs to Be a Priority for Ottawa." *Vancouver Sun*. Pacific Newspaper Group, 24 June 2015. Web. 20 July 2015. <http://www.vancouversun.com/news/Editorial fairness needs priority Ottawa/11164069/story.html>.

Edmonds, Richard L. *Taiwan in the Twentieth Century: A Retrospective View*. Cambridge: Cambridge UP, 2001. Print.

Evans, Anthony A., and David Gibbons. *The Illustrated Timeline of World War II*. New York, NY: Rosen Pub., 2012. Print.

Fan, Joshua. *China's Homeless Generation: Voices from the Veterans of the Chinese Civil War, 1940s-1990s*. Milton Park, Abingdon, Oxon: Routledge, 2011. Print.

Gale, Esson M. "Beachheads and Land Barriers of China." *Quarterly Review of the Michigan Alumnus* 51 (1944): 104-05. Print.

Ginsburg, Norton S. "Manchurian Railway Development." *The Far Eastern Quarterly* 8.4 (1949): 398-411. *Http://www.jstor.org/stable/2049540*. 1949. Web. 12 May 2014.

Hall, Andrew. "Constructing a 'Manchurian' Identity: Japanese Education in Manchukuo, 1931-1945." *ProQuest Dissertations and Theses*. (Order No. 3144935, University of Pittsburgh) (2003): 1-347. Print.

Halsema, James J. "1940 Japan-America Student Conference Diary." *KU ScholarWorks*. Publications of the Center for East Asian Studies, University of Kansas, Web. 16 May 2014.

"Harry S Truman, "Statement on Formosa," January 5, 1950." *USC US-China Institute*. University of Southern California, 25 Feb. 2014. Web. 11 May 2015. <http://china.usc.edu/harry-s-truman-"statement-formosa"-january-5-1950>.

Heinzig, Dieter. *The Soviet Union and Communist China 1945-1950: The Arduous Road to the Alliance*. Armonk, N.Y.: M.E. Sharpe, 2004. Print.

Henckaerts, Jean. *The International Status of Taiwan in the New World Order: Legal and Political Considerations*. London: Kluwer Law International, 1996. Print.

"History of Canadian Immigration Policy: Canadian Geographic Magazine January/February 2001." *Canadian Geographic Magazine*. 2001. Web. 21 July 2015. <http://www.canadiangeographic.ca/magazine/jf01/culture_acts.asp>.

Ho, Feng-Chiao, and Grace Chen. *The Reminiscences of Huang Tian-Hen*. Taipei,

Taiwan: Academia Historica, 2008. Print. (In Chinese)

Ho, Mingxiu. *Working-class Formation in Taiwan: Fractured Solidarity in State-owned Enterprises, 1945-2012.* New York: Palgrave Macmillan, 2014. Print.

Hooton, E. R. *The Greatest Tumult: The Chinese Civil War, 1936-49.* London: Brassey's, 1991. Print.

Hou, Elaine. "Exhibition on Canadian Missionary Mackay Opens in Taipei." *Exhibition on Canadian Missionary Mackay Opens in Taipei | Culture | Focus Taiwan—CNA English News.* Focus Taiwan, 16 Dec. 2014. Web. 18 Mar. 2015. <http://focustaiwan.tw/news/aedu/201412160030.aspx>.

House, Jonathan M. *A Military History of the Cold War, 1944-1962.* Norman, OK: U of Oklahoma, 2012. Print.

"House of Commons Procedure and Practice." 2009. Web. 1 June 2015. <http://www.parl.gc.ca/procedure-book-livre/Document.aspx?Language= E&Mode=1&sbdid=1B08A55C-743C-47DB-92E0-898D41340504 &sbpid=77160C1A-3FFA-4793-8B4D-41987000E6D4#_ftn9>.

Hsu, Hsueh-Chi. "Activities of Overseas Taiwanese During Japanese Colonization—Taiwanese Physicians in Manchuria." *Taiwan Historical Research* 11.2 (2004): 1-75 (in Chinese). Print.

Hsu, Hsueh-chi. *Taiwanese Experiences in Manchuria during the Japan Occupation.* Taipei, Taiwan: Institute of Modern History, Academia Sinica, 2002. Print. Text is in Chinese. Alternate citation: Xu, Xueji, and Xueji Xu. Ri zhi shi qi zai "Manzhou" de Taiwan ren. Chu ban. ed. Taibei Shi: Zhong yang yan jiu yuan jin dai shi yan jiu suo, 912002. Print.

Isom, Dallas Woodbury. *Midway Inquest Why the Japanese Lost the Battle of Midway.* Bloomington, IN: Indiana UP, 2007. Print.

Itoh, Mayumi. *Japanese War Orphans in Manchuria: Forgotten Victims of World War II.* New York, NY: Palgrave Macmillan, 2010. Print.

Itō, Takeo. *Life along the South Manchurian Railway: The Memoirs of Itō Takeo.* Armonk, N.Y.: M.E. Sharpe, 1988. Print.

Jang, Brent. "Vancouver Residents Blame Foreign Buyers for Housing Prices: Survey." *The Globe and Mail.* 18 June 2015. Web. 20 July 2015. <http://www.theglobeandmail.com/report-on-business/economy/housing/ vancouver-residents-blame-foreign-buyers-for-housing-prices-survey/ article25011087/>.

Jones, Francis Clifford. *Manchuria since 1931.* London: Royal Institute of International Affairs, 1949. Print.

Jones, W. J. "Manchuria's Development. II. Port Arthur." *Paperpast.* Oamaru Mail, 26 Nov. 1909. Web. 5 May 2014.

Jukes, Geoffrey. *The Russo-Japanese War 1904-1905.* Oxford: Osprey, 2002. Print.

Kaplan, David E. *Fires of the Dragon: Politics, Murder, and the Kuomintang*. New York: Atheneum, 1992. Print.

Katz, Paul R. *Religion and the Formation of Taiwanese Identities*. New York: Palgrave Macmillan, 2003. Print.

Katz, Paul R. *When Valleys Turned Blood Red: The Ta-pa-ni Incident in Colonial Taiwan*. Honolulu: U of Hawai'i, 2005. Print.

Kennedy, David M. *Freedom from Fear the American People in World War II*. Volume 2 ed. Oxford: Oxford U, 2004. Print.

Kerr, Gordon. *A Short History of China: From Ancient Dynasties to Economic Powerhouse*. Harpenden, Herts: Pocket Essentials, 2013. Print.

Kingsberg, Miriam. "The Poppy and the Acacia: Opium and Imperialism in Japanese Dairen and the Kwantung Leased Territory, 1905-1945." *ProQuest Dissertations and Theses* Order No. 3369090, University of California, Berkeley (2009): 1-422. Print.

Kuo, Adam. "More Overseas Taiwanese Repatriating: OCAC." *Www.ChinaPost.com.tw*. 22 Nov. 2013. Web. 20 July 2015. <http://www.chinapost.com.tw/taiwan/foreign-affairs/2013/11/22/394233/More-overseas.htm>.

Kuo, Cheng. *Global Competitiveness and Industrial Growth in Taiwan and the Philippines*. Pittsburgh: U of Pittsburgh, 1995. Print.

Kuo, Cheng-tian. *Religion and Democracy in Taiwan*. Albany, NY: State U of New York, 2008. Print.

Kuramoto, Kazuko. *Manchurian Legacy Memoirs of a Japanese Colonist*. East Lansing, Mich.: Michigan State UP, 1999. Print.

Kushner, Barak. *The Thought War Japanese Imperial Propaganda*. Honolulu: U of Hawaii, 2006. Print.

Lai, H. Mark. *Chinese American Transnational Politics*. Urbana: U of Illinois, 2010. Print.

Lan, Shi-Chi Mike. "The Ambivalence of National Imagination: Defining 'The Taiwanese' in China, 1931-1941." *The China Journal* No. 64 (2010): Pp. 179-197. *The University of Chicago Press on Behalf of the College of Asia and the Pacific, The Australian National University*. The University of Chicago Press. Web. 11 May 2015.

Lee, Chen-hsiang. *The Road to Freedom: Taiwan's Postwar Human Rights Movement*. Taipei: Dr Chen Wen-chen Memorial Foundation (Taiwan), 2004. Print.

Lee, Chong. *Counterinsurgency in Manchuria: The Japanese Experience, 1931-1940*. Santa Monica, Calif.: Rand, 1967. Print.

Lee, Shyu-tu, and Jack F. Williams. *Taiwan's Struggle: Voices of the Taiwanese*. Lanham, Maryland: Rowman and Littlefield, 2014. Print.

Ley, David. *Millionaire Migrants: Trans-Pacific Life Lines*. Chichester, U.K.: Wiley-Blackwell, 2010. Print.

Li, Xiaobing. *China at War an Encyclopedia*. Santa Barbara, Calif.: ABC-CLIO, 2012. Print.

Lin, Irene. "Taipei accuses China of exploiting quake." *Taipei Times*. 25 Sept. 1999. Web. 17 May 2017. <http://www.taipeitimes.com/News/front/archi ves/1999/09/25/0000003912>.

Lin, Sylvia Li. *Representing Atrocity in Taiwan: The 2/28 Incident and White Terror in Fiction and Film*. New York: Columbia UP, 2007. Print.

Lo, Ming. "Taiwanese Doctors under Japanese Rule." *Doctors within Borders Profession, Ethnicity, and Modernity in Colonial Taiwan*. Berkeley, Calif.: U of California, 2002. 1-24. Print.

Lohr, Steve. "Taiwan Convicts 2 in US Killing." *The New York Times*. The New York Times, 8 Apr. 1985. Web. 1 June 2015. <http://www.nytimes. com/1985/04/09/world/taiwan-convicts-2-in-u-s-killing.html>.

Low, Morris. "Doctors, Disease, and Development: Engineering Colonial Public Health in Southern Manchuria, 1905-1926; Robert John Perrins." *Building a Modern Japan: Science, Technology, and Medicine in the Meiji Era and beyond*. New York, NY: Palgrave Macmillan, 2005. 103-132. Print.

Lu, Hsiu-lien, and Ashley Esarey. *My Fight for a New Taiwan One Woman's Journey from Prison to Power*. Seattle, Washington: U of Washington, 2014. Print.

MacGregor, Mary Esther Miller. *The Black Bearded Barbarian; the Life of George Leslie Mackay of Formosa*. New York: Missionary Education Movement of the United States and Canada, 1912. Print.

Mackay, George Leslie, and J. A. Macdonald. *From Far Formosa: The Island, Its People and Missions*. Boston, Mass. Elibron Classics, 2005. Print.

Manthorpe, Jonathan. *Forbidden Nation: A History of Taiwan*. New York: Palgrave Macmillan, 2005. Print.

Maruyama, Paul. *Escape from Manchuria*. S.l.: Iuniverse, 2010. Print.

Mitter, Rana. *Forgotten Ally: China's World War II, 1937-1945*. New York: Houghton Mifflin Harcourt, 2013. Print.

Morii, Yusuke. *War and Medicine: Exhibition Panel Brochure: Facts and Responsibility of Participation of Japanese Medical Establishment in 15 Years' War: Project Exhibition in the 27th General Assembly of the Japan Medical Congress*. Osaka: Executive Committee of the Exhibition on War and Medicine 2007. Print.

Pagnamenta, Peter, and Momoko Williams. *Falling Blossom: A British Officer's Enduring Love for a Japanese Woman*. London: Century, 2006. Print.

Peng, Mingmin. *A Taste of Freedom; Memoirs of a Formosan Independence Leader.* New York: Holt, Rinehart and Winston, 1972. Print.

Pepper, Suzanne. *Civil War in China: The Political Struggle, 1945-1949.* 2nd ed. Lanham, Md.: Roman & Littlefield, 1999. Print.

Pew, Research. "Chapter 2. Views of Immigration." *Pew Research Centers Global Attitudes Project RSS.* 4 Oct. 2007. Web. 20 July 2015. <http://www.pewglobal.org/2007/10/04/chapter-2-views-of-immigration/>.

"Population Estimates Richmond 2014 Highlights and Summary Table." *British Columbia and Sub-Provincial.* Statistics Canada, Web. 20 July 2015. <http://www.bcstats.gov.bc.ca/StatisticsBySubject/Demography/Population Estimates.aspx>.

Ramzy, Austin. "Kenya Angers Taiwan by Deporting More Fraud Suspects to China." *The New York Times.* 09 Aug. 2016. Web. 17 May 2017. <http://www.nytimes.com/2016/08/09/world/asia/china-kenya-taiwan-deported.html>.

Rigger, Shelley. *Why Taiwan Matters: Small Island, Global Powerhouse.* Lanham: Rowman & Littlefield, 2011. Print.

Ring, Trudy. *International Dictionary of Historic Places.* London: Routledge, Taylor & Francis Group, 1995. Print.

Roy, Denny. *Taiwan: A Political History.* 1. Print ed. Ithaca, NY Cornell U, 2003. Print.

Rubinstein, Murray A. *The Other Taiwan: 1945 to the Present.* Armonk, N.Y.: M.E. Sharpe, 1994. Print.

Rubinstein, Murray A. *Taiwan: A New History.* Expanded ed. Armonk (N.Y.): M.E.Sharpe, 2007. Print.

Ruoff, Kenneth J. *Imperial Japan at Its Zenith: The Wartime Celebration of the Empire's 2,600th Anniversary.* Ithaca: Cornell UP, 2010. Print.

Rusbridger, James, and Eric Nave. *Betrayal at Pearl Harbor: How Churchill Lured Roosevelt into World War II.* New York: Summit, 1991. Print.

"San Francisco Peace Treaty." Taiwan Documents Project, 8 Sept. 1951. Web. 11 May 2015. <http://www.taiwandocuments.org/sanfrancisco01.htm>.

Scherer, Anke. "Japanese Emigration to Manchuria: Local Activists and the Making of the Village-Division Campaign." *Ruhr-Universitat Bochum 2006 Dissertation.* N.p., n.d. Web. 15 May 2014.

Shapiro, Fred R. *The Yale Book of Quotations.* New Haven: Yale UP, 2006. Print.

Shiba, Ryotaro, and Phyllis Birnbaum. *Clouds above the Hill a Historical Novel of the Russo-Japanese War, Volume 3.* Hoboken: Taylor and Francis, 2013. Print.

Skya, Walter. "Introduction." *Japan's Holy War: The Ideology of Radical Shintō Ultranationalism.* Durham: Duke UP, 2009. 1-32. Print.

Steele, Brent J., and Jonathan Acuff. *Theory and Application of the "generation" in*

International Relations and Politics. New York: Palgrave Macmillan, 2012. Print.

Suleski, Ronald Stanley. *The Modernization of Manchuria: An Annotated Bibliography.* Shatin, N.T., Hong Kong: Chinese UP, 1994. p. 25. Print.

Taiwan Communique. "The Murder of Henry Liu." *Http://www.taiwandc.org.* International Committee for Human Rights in Taiwan, 1 Apr. 1985. Web. 1 June 2015. <http://www.taiwandc.org/twcom/tc19-int.pdf>.

Tam, Pui-wing. "Chinatown Elders Of San Francisco Are At Odds Over Taiwan." *WSJ.* Wall Street Journal, 20 Apr. 2004. Web. 21 July 2015. <http://www.wsj.com/articles/SB108241541311087131>.

Tamanoi, Mariko. *Memory Maps the State and Manchuria in Postwar Japan.* Honolulu: U of Hawaii, 2009. Print.

Tang, Didi. "'Rotten banana': Chinese news service uses racist slur in 'shameless' editorial on departing US ambassador." *National Post.* Associated Press, 28 Feb. 2014. Web. 17 May 2017. <http://news.nationalpost.com/news/rotten-banana-chinese-news-service-uses-racist-slur-in-shameless-editorial-on-departing-u-s-ambassador>.

Tanner, Harold Miles. *The Battle for Manchuria and the Fate of China Siping, 1946.* Indianopolis: Indiana UP, 2013. Print.

"The History of Metropolitan Vancouver—1966 Chronology." *The History of Metropolitan Vancouver—1966 Chronology.* Web. 20 July 2015. <http://www.vancouverhistory.ca/chronology1966.htm>.

"The Republic of China Yearbook: Geography and Demographics." *-Geography & Demographics.* Executive Yuan, R.O.C. (Taiwan), 2014. Web. 25 Jan. 2015. <http://www.ey.gov.tw/en/cp.aspx?n=5776024635D354A6>.

Tiedemann, R. G. *Reference Guide to Christian Missionary Societies in China from the Sixteenth to the Twentieth Century.* Armonk, N.Y.: M.E. Sharpe, 2009. Print.

Tong, Hollington Kong. *Christianity in Taiwan: A History.* 2nd ed. Taipei: Printed by China Post, 1972. Print.

"Treaty of Friendship, Alliance and Mutual Assistance between the Union of Soviet Socialist Republics and the People's Republic of China." *The World and Japan" Database Project: Database of Japanese Politics and International Relations.* Institute of Oriental Culture, University of Tokyo, 14 Feb. 1950. Web. 11 May 2015. <http://www.ioc.u-tokyo.ac.jp/~worldjpn/documents/texts/docs/19500214.T1E.html>.

Tsai, Shih-Shan Henry. *Maritime Taiwan: Historical Encounters with the East and the West.* Armonk, N.Y.: M.E. Sharpe, 2009. P. 141. Print.

Van Der Wees, Gerrit. "Kaohsiung Incident a Good Reminder." *Taipeitime.com.*

Taipei Times, 9 Dec. 2009. Web. 1 June 2015. <http://www.taipeitimes.com/News/editorials/archives/2009/12/09/2003460513/1>.

Van Dyk, Lindsay. "Canadian Museum of Immigration at Pier 21." *Canadian Immigration Acts and Legislation*. Web. 20 July 2015. <http://www.pier21.ca/research/immigration-history/canadian-immigration-acts-and-legislation>.

Wachman, Alan. *Why Taiwan? Geostrategic Rationales for China's Territorial Integrity*. Stanford, Calif.: Stanford UP, 2007. Print.

Wickberg, Edgar. "Global Chinese Migrants and Performing Chineseness." *Journal of Chinese Overseas* (2007): 177-93. Print.

Wu, Der-yuan. "China Papers No. 9: Bridging "Forbidden" and "True North" Nations: Taiwan's Agency in Canada's China Policy." *Opencanada.org*. Canadian International Council, 1 Mar. 2010. Web. 1 June 2015. <http://opencanada.org/wp-content/uploads/2011/05/Taiwans-Agency-in-Canadas-China-Policy-Der-yuan-Wu.pdf>.

Wu, Micha. *A History of Taiwan in Comics*. All New Ed., [Chinese-English ed. Taiwan: Third Nature, 2004. Print.

Wu, Zhuoliu, and Duncan B. Hunter. *The Fig Tree: Memoirs of a Taiwanese Patriot, 1900-1947*. Dortmund: Prokekt Verlag, 1994. Print.

Xu, Xueji, and Xueji Xu. *Ri Zhi Shi Qi Zai "Manzhou" De Taiwan Ren*. Chu Ban. ed. Taibei Shi: Zhong Yang Yan Jiu Yuan Jin Dai Shi Yan Jiu Suo, 912002. Print. based on ISBN 957-671-844-9

Young, C. Walter. *Japan's Special Position in Manchuria; Its Assertion, Legal Interpretation and Present Meaning*. Baltimore: Johns Hopkins. 1931. Print.

Young, Ian. "Rich Chinese Immigrants' Deception Costs British Columbia Billions." *South China Morning Post*. SCMP Group Limited, 9 Oct. 2014. Web. 20 July 2015. <http://www.scmp.com/news/world/article/1612403/rich-chinese-immigrants-deception-costs-british-columbia-billions?page=all>.

Young, Louise. *Japan's Total Empire Manchuria and the Culture of Wartime Imperialism*. Berkeley: U of California, 1998. Print.

Zarrow, Peter Gue. *China in War and Revolution, 1895-1949*. London: Routledge, 2005. Print.

Zepetnek, Steven, and Yiu-nam Leung. *Canadian Culture and Literature: And a Taiwan Perspective*. Edmonton: Research Institute for Comparative Literature, U of Alberta. 1998. Print.

Notes

CHAPTER I

1. Suleski p. 25

2. Dr Takayama worked for the Ministry of Health and was employed part-time by the school.

3. May 5 is Boys' Day.

4. Hsu *Taiwan Historical Research* p. 66-67

5. Shinkyō later reverted to its original Chinese name, Changchun (長春), after the Second World War.

6. Chou (abstract)

7. Ibid.

8. Lo p. 6

9. Hsu (English abstract)

10. Tsai p. 141

11. Rusbridger

12. The oldest boy, 正昭, became Akihisa (明久) and the second boy, 正義, became Tadahisa (忠久). He also transformed himself from Jin Han (金涵) to Naoya (直也) and his wife from Lin Chou (林綢) to Shuko (周子). To the youngest children he gave only Japanese names, a sign of his faith in the continuing strength of the Japanese Empire. The girl was called Kazuko (和子) and the youngest boy Yukihisa (幸久.) It was only later, when circumstances had changed, that the youngest children acquired their Chinese names, 榮華 and 正幸.

13. The seven-five-three festival (odd numbers are considered lucky by the Japanese) commemorates girls aged three and seven and boys aged three and five. Prayers are said at Shinto shrines to keep the children safe from evil spirits.

Rites of passage include allowing three-old girls to grow out their hair, five-year-old boys to begin wearing *hakama* (a skirt worn by Japanese men), and seven-year-old girls to start wearing *obi* (a sash for the kimono) instead of a rope around their waists. It's believe that the custom began among the samurai class and spread to commoners during the Edo period.

CHAPTER 2

1. Jukes p. 60

The battle at 203-Metre Hill was a crucial Japanese victory in the Russo-Japanese War. To take 203-Metre Hill, "the cost to the Japanese was 14,000 dead, including almost all of 7th Division . . . An observation post was placed on the hill on 6 December, and in two days shells from the siege guns directed from the hill had all the [Russian] battleships except the *Sevastopol* sitting on the mud of the harbor bottom."

2. The New Education Movement, in vogue during the Taisho Period (1912-1926), emphasized a child-centred approach to education in contrast to the Confucian system that was in place prior to the reform. The movement lost favour when militaristic ultranationalists came to power in the 1930s and 40s.

3. Skya p. 12

4. Hall p. 300

5. Ibid.

6. Hall p. 301

7. Cull p. 444

8. Morii p. 40

9. Jones

10. Gale p. 104

11. Jones

"The youthful Chinese living in the vicinity earn an occasional half-dollar by selling the tourist such articles as are to be picked upon on the battlefield. A Chinese boy who had been combing the hills for treasure with a three-pronged fork pulled from his open shirt front an unexploded Gatling gun shell and offered it to us for a small consideration, but Mr Irida, shouting "Abunai!" (Danger!) hurried us away. Our guide subsequently explained that the Chinese do not appear to appreciate the consequences of indiscriminately handling unexploded shells and often come to grief on that account. When 203-Metre Hill was captured a shell was placed on the top of a five-foot base, and this served to give the direction to the Japanese gunners on the hill opposite, who had been wasting ammunition in an attempt to locate the enemy's fleet in the harbor. At the end of four days' bombardment the Russian ships were put out of action."

12. Ruoff p. 132

13. Tamanoi p. 1

14. Itō p. 14

15. Itō p. 15

16. Itō p. 14-15

17. Itō p. 9

18. Scherer p. 1
19. Maruyama p. 1
Also from the Introduction:
"Of the Japanese on the Chinese mainland, approximately 1.7 million appeared to have been in Manchuria."
20. Ginsburg p. 398
21. Russian meaning: the faraway place
22. Kuramoto p. 20, Low p. 111
23. Birnbaum p. 367
24. Low p. 111
25. The name of the Liaotung Peninsula under Japanese rule.
26. Culver p. 18
27. Kuramoto p. 19
28. Ibid.
29. Culver p. 18
30. The Battle of Mukden was the final battle in the Russo-Japanese War and the largest land battle ever fought before the onset of World War One. Akihisa would have traced part of the route from Port Arthur to Mukden in reverse during his field study.
31. Ruoff p. 9
32. Ruoff p. 134
33. Shiba p. 68
"The rendering of the hill's name was brilliant. In this, Nogi displayed a poetic gift that is truly sublime. The figure 203, which marks the height of the hill, can be read in Japanese *ni-rei-san*. Using Chinese characters with the same pronunciations but different meanings, he recast the hill's name as 'hill of thy spirits.' This is no mere play on words but a fitting tribute in only three characters to the souls of the uncountable numbers who perished on the hill, including Nogi's own son Yasusuke. The poem ends by intoning again, 'hill of thy spirits.'" The poem translated from classical Chinese:

> 203 hill, though steep, is not impossible to climb.
> Men know that to obtain glory they must overcome obstacles.
> Covered in blood and iron, the hill scarcely retains its shape.
> All look up with deep emotion at the hill where thy spirits lie.

Another translation (Pagnamenta p. 44):

> The 203 metre hill, steep though it may be
> Is surely not climbable
> Young men know perils need to be overcome
> If glory is to be won
> Bullets fall and blood pours
> And the hill changes shape
> Look up and pray to the mountain
> Where your spirits rest.

34. Information from tourist plaque on 203-Metre Hill.

35. Isom p. 38; Nelson's signal to the fleet: England expects that every man will do his duty." Shapiro p. 548

CHAPTER 3

1. Jones, Francis p. 221-223

2. Kuramoto p. 44

3. Also known as the Mukden Incident. The Manchurian Incident was the trigger for the Second Sino-Japanese War. On September 18, 1931, a small explosion occurred on a section of the railway near Mukden owned by the South Manchurian Railway Company. The Japanese government accused Chinese dissidents of sabotage and used it as an excuse to invade Manchuria. Manchukuo was established six months later. It is widely believed that the explosion was staged by the Japanese military.

4. Kennedy p. 393

5. Kushner p. 34

6. Jones p. 247

7. Hsu (aka Xu) p. 525 as told by 陳嘉樹 (in Chinese)

8. Hsu (aka Xu) p. 527-529

9. Hsu (aka Xu) p. 472-474

10. Young, Louise p. 183

11. Jones, FC p. 230

12. Lee, Chong p. xi

13. Kuramoto p. 52

14. Russian word for "watch."

15. 新京, the Japanese name for the capital of Manchukuo; now Changchun (长春), China

16. Hsu (aka Xu) p. 595 as told by 許長卿 (in Chinese)

17. Hsu (aka Xu) p. 112

18. Hsu (aka Xu) p. 17

CHAPTER 4

1. Kerr p. 119-121

2. Yuan died from uremia at the age of fifty-six.

3. Hooton p.xxvi

4. Chiang had taken over the Kuomintang after Sun Yat-Sen's death in 1925 at the age of 58 from liver cancer.

5. Sun had planned this expedition before his untimely death.

6. One of these was the Manchurian warlord Zhang Zuolin who controlled all of Manchuria as well as some northern provinces. (Dillon p. 192)

7. Also known as the April 12 Incident.

8. Kerr p. 126

9. Kerr p. 123-130, Dillon p. 188-217

10. Like the Manchurian Incident, the Marco Polo Bridge Incident is believed by some historians to have been staged by the Japanese as a pretext for invasion. In July 1937, the Chinese and Japanese clashed when the Japanese, conducting military exercises in the area of the Marco Polo Bridge (a stone structure in Beijing), wanted to search Chinese territory near Beijing for a missing Japanese soldier. When the Chinese refused, all-out conflict ensued, marking the start of the Second Sino-Japanese War.

11. Dillon p. 249

12. Pepper p. xi-xiii

13. Hooton p. 23

14. Tanner p. 56

15. Marshall is better known as the architect of the Marshall Plan for postwar European recovery.

16. Dillon p. 251. The Communist forces officially became the People's Liberation Army on May 1, 1946.

17. Kerr p. 133

18. House p. 154

19. Mitter p. 269

20. 漢奸, literally "traitor to the Han race"

21. Kuramoto p. 103

CHAPTER 5

1. Pepper p. 26

2. Pepper p. 14

3. Pepper p. 15

4. Loh p. 9

5. Xu p. 118

6. 長沼公園

7. Xu p. 595

8. Kuramoto p. 111

9. Chan, Foreword

10. Morii p. 42-45

11. Morii p. 43

12. Morii p. 91

13. Morii p. 7

14. 吳三連, Wu San Lian

15. 楊肇加, Yang Zhao Jia. Both the Tianjin and Shanghai Taiwanese Association presidents were later politically active in Taiwan.

16. Xu p. 90

CHAPTER 6

1. Yongkang District (永康)

2. Davidson, various chapters

3. Kuo, Cheng p. 54

4. Edmunds p. 49

5. Rubenstein (The Other Taiwan) p. 4

6. Fan p. 11-12

7. Fan p. 12-13

8. Rubenstein (The Other Taiwan) p. 4

9. Cheng-Chao would call him Tadahisa throughout his life.

10. 井戸端会議

11. Wu p. 24

12. The Republic of China Yearbook

13. Amis 阿美, Atayal 泰雅, Bunun 布農, Kavalan 噶瑪蘭, Paiwan 排灣, Puyuma 卑南, Rukai 魯凱, Saisiyat 賽夏, Sakizaya 撒奇萊雅, Seediq (or Sediq) 賽德克, Thao 邵, Truku 太魯閣, Tsou 鄒, Yami 雅美 (or Dawu 達悟), Hlaalua 拉阿魯哇 and Kanakanavu 卡那卡那富; the three largest groups—the Amis, the Paiwan and the Atayal—accounted for 70.78 percent of the indigenous population. (From The Republic of China Yearbook)

14. Davidson p. 8

15. Zarrow p. 343

16. 童乩 "dang gi" in Taiwanese

17. *Scomberomorus commerson*, 塗魠魚

18. *budaixi* in Mandarin or *pò-tē-hì* in Taiwanese, 布袋戲

19. The real time puppet show called The Scholar Swordsman: Shi Yan-wen (雲州大儒俠 — 史艷文) was developed by Huang Chun-hsiung (黃俊雄), son of renowned puppet master Huang Hai-tai (黃海岱); Katz p. 107.

CHAPTER 7

1. Wang Yude 王育德

2. Chou et al p. 315

3. Roy p. 63

4. Wu, Z p. 133

5. Ring p. 794

6. Wu, Z p. 131

7. Ta-pa-ni incident of 1915 in Tainan county, Katz 2005

8. Rubenstein (Taiwan: A New History) p. 247

9. Chou et al p. 317-318; Roy p. 67-68; Wu p. 132

10. Chou et al p. 319-320; Roy p. 67-68; Wu, Z p. 133; Manthorpe p. 192-193

11. Manthorpe p. 192

12. Manthorpe p. 192; Roy p. 68

13. Roy p. 69

14. Known as the Thirty-Two Demands

15. Manthorpe p. 193

16. Roy p. 71

17. Fan p. 15

18. Lee C-h p. 101-103

19. Fan p. 16
20. Manthorpe p. 193
21. Roy p. 71
22. Fan p. 16; Roy p. 73
23. Manthorpe p. 193
24. "About three thousand Taiwanese dissidents fled the island." Roy p. 73
25. 王育霖
26. 民生公園; now the Tang Dezhang Memorial Park, 湯德章紀念公園
27. Ho, F-C p. 187; Lee C-h p. 92
28. Chen Yi was recalled and promoted to governor of Zhejiang province on the mainland in May, 1947 but beheaded by Chiang a few years later for treason. Manthorpe, p. 194, Ring p. 794
29. Manthorpe p. 194
30. Bedford p. 38
31. Dreyer p. 381
32. Lee, C-h p. 21
33. Chiang died on April 5, 1975.
34. Roy p. 85
35. Chou et al p. 333, Roy p. 78
36. Li p. 395
37. Martial law "lasted from May 20, 1949 until July 14, 1987." Fan p. 16
38. Ho, M p. 51
39. Lee, C-h p. 18 and p. 41
40. Chou et al p. 333
41. Lin, S p. 4; Chou et al p. 333, 339; Lee C-h p. 18
42. Lin, S p. 5
43. Roy p. 91
44. The legislation was called "Temporary Provisions Effective During the Period of Communist Rebellion." Roy p. 83
45. Lee C-h p. 44
46. Chou et al p. 336
47. Manthorpe p. 204
48. Lee C-h p. 26-27
49. Lee C-h p. 28
50. Lee C-h p. 111
51. Roy p. 79
52. Lee C-h p. 26
53. Manthorpe p. 184; Roy p. 111
54. Chou et al p. 352

CHAPTER 8

1. 天馬, Pegasus Café
2. 中華日報, *Zhonghua ribao*, China Daily, a KMT newspaper
3. 王大樹

4. 陳章哲, a physician who practiced in Dalian

5. 大連宏済醫院 had 40-50 beds and 400-500 outpatients a day.

6. 王愛真

7. Tiedemann p. 5-8

8. Knox College in Toronto, Princeton Seminary, and New College in Edinburgh.

9. MacGregor Chapter IV

10. Hou

11. Now Tamkang Middle School.

12. Aletheia University

13. Forsberg p. 3

14. Zepetnek p. 73

15. Zepetnek p. 73; Forsberg p. 3

16. Minnie Mackay and GLM married in 1878.

17. Issued in 2001 to mark the centenary of Mackay's death.

18. Hōklo, Hakka, and the various aborigine languages.

19. 一貫道. A Chinese religious sect also known as the Persistent Way or the Way of Unity which combined elements from Confucianism, Taoism, Buddhism, and shamanism. The sect grew in popularity throughout the 1930s and 40s on the Mainland with millions of followers. In Taiwan, the movement drew thousands of new believers even after the religion was banned.

20. Lee C-h p. 27

21. 重男, 轻女

22. 關係

CHAPTER 9

1. はいぶつりよう, to reuse and recycle

2. The government assigned men between the ages of 18 and 36 to either two years of service in the army or three years in the navy or air force. The length of service has been now decreased and service is being shifted from compulsory to voluntary.

3. Exams were administered from 1954 to 1976. Barkan p. 1331

4. 本省人, native province people

5. 外省人, out of province people

6. Also known as the "Hart Celler Act."

7. Barkan p. 1332

8. Lee C-h p. 27

9. Cairo Conference Press Release

10. San Francisco Peace Treaty, Article 23

11. Chi essay

12. Lan p. 184

13. Roy p. 108

14. Lan p. 187-188

15. Lan p. 191

16. Wachman p. 79
17. Manthorpe p. 194
18. Roy p. 113

CHAPTER 10

1. Henckaerts p. 66
2. Tsai p. 191
3. Wu, M p. 15
4. Now called the Taipei Economic and Cultural Office (TECO).
5. "New York, Los Angeles, Chicago, San Francisco, Boston, Houston, Atlanta, Seattle, and Honolulu." Tsai p. 197
6. Even before Canada's official recognition of the PRC, Canadian relations with Taiwan were "friendly but not intimate." Canada had never set up embassies in Taiwan despite the presence of Taiwanese consulates in Canada. TECO offices were established in Toronto and Vancouver in 1991, years after the 1970 breaking off of official ties between Canada and Taiwan. Wu D p. 2
7. The photograph would appear on page A3 of the Sunday, January 27, 1980 edition of the paper.
8. The Taiwanese Association, 台灣同鄉會, eventually grew to twenty branches of across Canada and is still active today.
9. Several Taiwanese students had been targeted by the KMT over alleged anti-government activities ever since studies abroad were permitted. In 1966, Huang Qiming, a doctoral student at the University of Wisconsin was arrested and sentenced to five years in prison for attending Taiwanese independence meetings. Another graduate student, Chen Yuxi, was accused of reading Communist literature at a University of Hawaii library and initially sentenced to death by a military court. In 1978, Rita Yeh, a student of social sciences at the University of Minnesota, was arrested upon her return to Taiwan and charged with planning to overthrow the government and spreading Communist propaganda. Chen's death sentence was reduced to seven years in prison after international pressure and he was released in 1971. Yeh would later be sentenced to fourteen years in prison for sedition. Lai pp. 41-42 and Chang, Iris p. 298
10. 黃文雄
11. 鄭自才
12. Lee C-h p. 112; Roy p. 166
13. Rubenstein (Taiwan: A New History) p. 438
14. Kuo C-t p. 39
15. Lee C-h p. 113
16. Lee C-h p. 142-150
17. Lu p. 109; Roy p. 167
18. The third issue sold 100,000 copies making *Meilidao* the second most popular magazine after the Taiwanese *TV Guide*. Lu p. 109
19. The "Kaoshiung Eight" included Chang Chun-hung, Huang Hsin-chieh, Chen Chu, Yao Chia-wen, Shih Ming-teh, Lin Hung-hsuan, Annette

Lu, and Lin Yi-hsiung.

20. Lin C-h p. 118, Lu Chapter 6

21. He is not certain if he was blacklisted before 1980 because he never tried to visit Taiwan in the 1960s and 70s.

22. The blacklist was apparently lifted in 1991, several years after the 1987 lifting of martial law. Lai p. 43

23. 陳文成

24. The security agency of the KMT.

25. Loa 2013

26. 劉宜良. Also known by his pen name Chiang Nan, 江南

27. 陳啟禮; nicknamed King Duck

28. Kaplan p. 369

29. Taiwan Communiqué p. 10

30. Kaplan p. 476-77

31. Lee S-t Chapter 16

32. Canadian Press

33. Lee S-t p. 162 Note 22

34. Lee S-t p. 127

35. Also true for Canadian parliament. See House of Commons Procedure and Practice Note 38

36. Culpan

CHAPTER 11

1. Editor, Vancouver Sun, June 24, 2015

2. The programme required applicants to have assets of at least $1.6 million and to provide $800,000 in loans to Canada. SCMP article: Young Oct 2014

3. Richmond, a former suburb of Vancouver, is considered part of the Greater Vancouver region.

4. Jang June 18, 2015

5. Ley p. 183-191

6. Van Dyk

7. Van Dyk

8. History of Canadian Immigration Policy

9. Of 67,095 identified Taiwanese, 53750 had arrived between 1991 and 2001; History of Canadian Immigration Policy

10. 蔡阿信, 1896-1990; Dong

11. Canadian Press 2013

12. It was one of Prime Minister Pierre Trudeau's major foreign relations initiatives.

13. Steele p. 128-129

14. Tam 2004

15. http://www.economist.com/blogs/dailychart/2011/11/diasporas

16. Wickberg p. 183

CHAPTER 12

1. 心疼, (pronounced um gum in Taiwanese) means to begrudge, usually referring to the loss of or hurt to a loved one

2. See link for part of the joke. http://board.jokeroo.com/funny-jokes/138924-george-carlin-aging.html

3. Current progress in Canadian courts regarding physician-assisted suicide can be found here: http://bccla.org/our_work/carter-et-al-v-attorney-general-of-canada-2/. American laws on physician-assisted suicides vary from state to state. As of 2017, California, Colorado, Montana, District of Columbia, Oregon, Vermont, and Washington have de-criminalized physician-assisted suicides.

4. Lin, I

5. Tang

6. Ramzy

Place Names

Current Name (simplified Chinese characters)	Name Under Qing Rule (traditional Chinese characters)	Name Under Japanese Rule (1932-45)	Notes
Changchun; 长春	Changchun; 長春 (literal meaning: long spring)	Shinkyō (新京) (literal meaning: new capital)	Capital of Jilin Province in northeast China. Was the capital of Manchukuo.
Dalian; 大连	Small fishing village called 青泥洼桥 taken over by the Russians in 1898 and renamed *Dal'nii*	Dairen (大連)	Major port city in Liaoning Province, China
Green Island Lüdao; 綠島			Island off the eastern coast of Taiwan where political prisoners served jail sentences during the White Terror
Kaohsiung; 高雄	Fonghan County; 鳳山縣	Takao; 高雄	Large port city in southwestern Taiwan
Keelung; 基隆			Major port in northeastern Taiwan near Taipei
Kinmen or Quemoy; 金門			Group of Taiwanese islands off the southeastern coast of China

Lüshun Port; 旅顺港	Lüshun Port; 旅顺港 Port Arthur; 亚瑟港	Ryojun (旅顺)	Southernmost point of Liaoning Province, China (one of the districts of Dalian)
Shanhaiguan; 山海关	Shan-hai-kuan; 山海關		One of the major passes in the Great Wall of China located 300 kilometres east of Beijing which leads to northeast China
Shenyang; 沈阳	1) Mukden (ᠮᡠᡴᡩᡝᠨ, derived from Manchurian word "to rise") 2) Fengtian, Fengtien, 奉天 (literal Chinese meaning "respect heaven") 3) Shenyang, 瀋陽 (Chinese name changed back to pre-Manchu name of Shenyang from Fengtian in 1914 then to Fengtian again under the Japanese)	Hōten (奉天)	Capital of Liaoning Province in northeast China. Site of 1931 Mukden Incident.
Tainan City	Capital city, 府城	Tainan *Shū* (臺南州)	Oldest city in Taiwan, located in the southwest of the island; former capital city
Tamsui; 淡水			Sea coast area in New Taipei. Other historical spellings: Tamshuy, Tamshui, Tamsoui, Tan-sui
Tieling; 铁岭	Tieling; 鐵嶺	Tetsurei (鐵嶺)	City in Liaoning Province in northeast China.
Yongkang District; 永康區			District in Tainan, Taiwan; site of Yang ancestral home
Xiamen; 厦门	Amoy; 廈門		Major city in China's Fujian province where Hokkien is spoken
Zhangzhou; *Chang-chou*; 漳州			City in Fujian province where Charles Yang's ancestors lived

Abridged List of People Named

The table is ordered by surnames, in accordance with Chinese custom, using spellings preferred by the individuals. Romanization of Communist Chinese names follow pinyin conventions and of Taiwanese names (and Chinese names before 1949) follow Wade-Giles or modified Wade-Giles in accordance with common usage at the time. Pinyin names are rendered in simplified Chinese characters and the remainder in traditional Chinese.

Wade-Giles or Modified Wade-Giles	Pinyin	Chinese Characters	Notes
Chen Yi (1883-1950)		陳儀	Garrison Commander of Taiwan after Japanese surrender post-WWII and presided over the 2-2-8 Incident; later executed by Chiang Kai-Shek for alleged plans to surrender to the Chinese Communists
Cheng Tzu-Tsai (1936-)		鄭自才	Member of World United Formosans for Independence involved in failed 1970 assassination attempt on Chiang Ching-Kuo
Chiang Ching-Kuo (1910-1988)		蔣經國	Son of Chiang Kai-Shek; Ruled Taiwan from his father's death to his own death in 1988

Chiang Kai-Shek (1887-1975)	Jiang Jieshi Jiang Zhongzheng	蔣介石 蔣中正	Leader of the Republic of China until retreat to Taiwan in 1949 after defeat in Chinese Civil War. Ruled Taiwan until his death in 1975
Huang Chun-hsiung (1933-)		黃俊雄	Well-known Taiwanese puppeteer, son of renowned Taiwanese puppeteer (黃海岱)
Huang, Peter/ Wen-shiung (1937-)		黃文雄	Member of World United Formosans for Independence involved in failed 1970 assassination attempt on Chiang Ching-Kuo
Kao Chun-ming (1929-)		高俊明	Taiwanese Presbyterian minister active in the democracy movement
Kaohsiung Eight: 1) Chang Chun-hung (1938-) 2) Chen Chu (1950-) 3) Huang Hsin-chieh (1928-1999) 4) Lin Hung-hsuan (1942- 2015) 5) Lin Yi-hsiung (1941-) 6) Lu, Annette/ Hsiu-lien (1944-) 7) Shih Ming-teh (1941-) 8) Yao Chia-wen (1938-)		1) 張俊宏 2) 陳菊 3) 黃信介 4) 林弘宣 5) 林義雄 6) 呂秀蓮 7) 施明德 8) 姚嘉文	Activists jailed for the 1979 Kaohsiung Incident
Koxinga (Lord of the Imperial Surname); Zheng Chenggong		國姓爺; 鄭成功	Ming loyalist who retreated to Taiwan, while resisting Qing rule, in the 1660s
Lee Teng-hui (1923-)		李登輝	Chairman of the Nationalist Party and President of the Republic of China from 1988-2000; first native-born Taiwanese to be president in Taiwan
Lin Yu-san (1924-)		林有杉	Retired pharmacist and Charles Yang's cousin. He was interviewed in August, 2014 at his home in Yongkang, Taiwan by the author.

	Mao Zedong (1893-1976)	毛泽东	Chairman of the Communist Party of China from 1949 until his death in 1976
Matzu, also Ma-tsu	Mazu	媽祖	Chinese goddess of the sea said to protect sailors; worshipped in China and Taiwan
Shirō Ishii (1892-1959)		石井 四郎	Japanese army doctor who directed the Ishii Network during WWII
Sun Yat-Sen (1866-1925)		孫逸仙	Founding father of Republic of China
Tai Li (1897-1946)	Dai Li	戴笠	Head of Chiang Kai-Shek's Military Intelligence Service until Li's death in a suspicious plane crash
Tang De-jhang (1907-1947)	Tang Dezhang	湯德章	Taiwanese politician executed during 2-2-8
Teacher Wang (1924-85)	Wang Yude	王育德 (Taiwanese pronunciation: Ong Iok-tek)	Taiwanese language scholar and independence leader; Charles Yang's high school teacher
Wei Tao-Ming (1899-1978)		魏道明	Republic of China ambassador to the US during WWII and first civilian governor of Taiwan
Wang Ai-chen (1932-2010)		王愛真	Charles Yang's wife, Jane Yang
Wang Ching-wei, a.k.a. Wang Chao-ming (1883-1944)	Wang Jingwei a.k.a. Wang Zhaoming	汪精衛 汪兆銘	Political rival of Chiang Kai-Shek within the Kuomintang who later established a collaborationist government with the Japanese; widely regarded as a traitor to the Chinese
Wang Da-shu (1905-1973)		王大樹	Charles Yang's father-in-law, a physician in Manchuria
Yang Jin Han (1908-1995)		楊金涵	Charles Yang's father; Japanese name: Naoya Takayama
Yuan Shih-kai (1859-1916)		袁世凱	Imperial War Minister during Qing dynasty who later became President of the Republic of China and self-proclaimed Emperor

Acknowledgments

The genesis for this book was a meeting with Ruey Satake (林瑞麟), past president of the Society of Taiwanese Canadian History in BC, where the idea for a biography-based account of modern Taiwanese history and emigration was first raised. I would like to thank members of the society for providing me with access to their archives, in particular Sam Lin (林聖崇) and Ben Tseng (曾立斌). Thanks also to Cecilia Chueh (陳慧中), director of the Taiwanese Canadian Cultural Society (TCCS) for providing me with materials related to the Taiwanese in Vancouver and introducing me to the TCCS library. And to Charlie Wu (吳權益) for including this book in the 2017 Taiwanfest events.

A note of appreciation to Allan Cho, Emily Lin, and Andre Hsu (許長謨) for research materials from the University of British Columbia; University of Nevada, Las Vegas; and various Taiwanese universities. Thanks also to Emily Cho for creating the maps of Asia.

Heartfelt thanks for time generously given for interviews by Peng Ming Min (彭明敏), Lin Yi-hsiung (林義雄), Koh Seikai (許世楷), Annette Lu (呂秀蓮), Su Huan-chih (蘇煥智), Lin Tai-hua (林岱樺), Ellen Huang (黃越綏), Yu-san Lin (林有杉), Wan-yao Chou (周婉窈), Ho Chie Tsai, and Jenny Wang (汪采羿). Thanks also to John Chou (周昭亮) for details about the 1980 Seattle protest. Charlie Smith's tips about interview techniques were much appreciated during the three years of research.

Thank you to the following for arranging interviews: Lucy Lu (盧月鉛), Michael Chou (周宏慶), Jenny Wong (汪寶真), Su Shiow-lan (蘇秀蘭) and my mother Lily Lin (陳麗嬌). Special thanks to my father Tom Lin (林頂義) for all his help throughout the research and interview process.

Genuine gratitude to readers of various drafts of the manuscript, namely Teresa Farn, Tracy Wong, Becky Ward, Gordon Wong, Wan-yao Chou (周婉窈), Alison Bailey, and Jonathan Manthorpe; with particular thanks to Alison Bailey, Wan-yao Chou, and Jonathan Manthorpe for writing "blurbs" for the book. And, of course, MG Vassanji's expert editing and Nurjehan Aziz's help were invaluable.

Most of all, I am obliged to Charles Yang for sharing his passion about the fate of Taiwan and for allowing his story to be publicized. I appreciate his valiant efforts to recall facts from his childhood. Where time has dimmed his memory, I have reconstructed events using research and deduction. I would also like to thank his extended family for their feedback on the manuscript, especially to Yu-san Lin for helping me fill in some of the gaps in Charles Yang's Manchurian memories.

In the writing of this book, I have endeavoured to be faithful to the truth and respectful of the views not only the Taiwanese but also those of other players in the global dramas played out during the nearly nine decades of Charles Yang's life. The dominant voice is, of course, his. While he speaks for many in the Taiwanese diaspora, there are differing views, even among the Taiwanese themselves, as he would be the first to acknowledge. Ultimately, this biography attempts to document the tumultuous history of a small island off the coast of China over the twentieth and twenty-first centuries through a personal lens and should be taken as the filtered and biased story that it is.

I am grateful for the opportunity to write this book because it has brought me closer to the land of my parents and I hope Charles Yang's story will serve as a bridge between generations and cultures for others as well.

Julia Lin

2017